Night Is Gone,
Day Is Still Coming

Night Is Gone,
Day Is Still Coming

STORIES AND POEMS BY
AMERICAN INDIAN TEENS AND YOUNG ADULTS

❊ ❊ ❊

EDITED BY
Annette Piña Ochoa, Betsy Franco, and Traci L. Gourdine

INTRODUCTION BY
Simon J. Ortiz

CANDLEWICK PRESS
CAMBRIDGE, MASSACHUSETTS

Introduction copyright © 2003 by Simon J. Ortiz
Poems, stories, and essays in this collection copyright © year of publication
as indicated in Acknowledgments.
This collection copyright © 2003 by Annette Piña Ochoa, Betsy Franco, and Traci L. Gourdine

FIRST EDITION 2003

Library of Congress Cataloging-in-Publication Data
Night is gone, day is still coming : stories and poems by American Indian teens and young
adults / edited by Annette Piña Ochoa, Betsy Franco, and Traci L. Gourdine;
introduction by Simon J. Ortiz
p. cm.
ISBN 0-7636-1518-8
1. American literature — Indian authors. 2. Indians of North America — Literary collections.
3. Indian teenagers — Literary collections. 4. Indian youth — Literary collections. 5. American
literature — 21st century. 6. Teenagers' writings, American. 7. Youths' writings, American.
I. Ochoa, Annette Piña. II. Franco, Betsy. III. Gourdine, Traci L.

PS508.I5 W47 2003
81.9'9283'08997 — dc21   2002074086

2 4 6 8 10 9 7 5 3 1

Printed in the United States of America

This book was typeset in 12/15 Bembo
Design by Lisa Clark

CANDLEWICK PRESS
2067 Massachusetts Avenue
Cambridge, Massachusetts 02140

visit us at www.candlewick.com

To my family and Maya: Thank you for being my voice.
And to all the other parents, whose children shared their voice with us.
Emillano with love.

A. P. O.

For Doug, who expands my world

B. F.

For my daughters Mara and Tyne

T. L. G.

Contents

Preface	*Annette Piña Ochoa*	*xi*
Introduction	*Simon J. Ortiz*	*xii*
Whispers	*Vincent F. White*	*1*
Summertime	*Patrick Lewis*	2
Subway Mourning	*Vena A-dae*	4
Red Light. Green Light.	*Gerri Lillian Williams*	6
"My heart was pounding . . ."	*Denise Marie Joaquin*	8
Showing Me	*Vena A-dae*	10
Camouflage	*Annette Bird Saunooke*	12
Disneyland	*Sara M. Ortiz*	14
The Dance	*Skylar Frank-Green Moser*	16
Red Girls	*Mary Redhouse*	18
The Crow Fair of Yesteryear	*Frederick M. Howe III*	19
Handsome Indian Boy	*Joanna M. Crazy Mule*	20
Berry Paints	*Mikel D. Brown*	21
Who Am I?	*Roger D. White Owl*	22
The Gap	*Thomas M. Yeahpau*	24
My Mind's Words	*Jorell "Space Man" X. LaBarge*	26
Butch's Drop	*Thomas M. Yeahpau*	28

Pouring Milk Before Cereal	Vena A-dae	33
"I remember the Vodka Summer . . ."	Nakesha Bradley	35
"Her blood runs proud . . ."	Carrie M. Brown	36
Untitled '96	Angela Damron	38
Butterfly Princess	Gerri Lillian Williams	39
Susto	Ayme Almendarez	42
Mom's Fry Bread	Lateachia Pemma	44
My Indian Pooh Bear	Beth Yana J. Pease	45
Neah Bay, Washington, to Me	Brandan T.N. McCarty	46
As I Looked	Katrina Perry	48
Grandma	Melvin Left Hand	49
Would You Cry?	Maria Lee Feather Brien	50
Dark Waters	Sonia Manriquez	51
"Dear Mother, . . ."	Anonymous	52
Young at Heart	Jody Roach	56
Grandparents	Dewey Bright Wings	58
rain inside the end of august	Lani Wild	59
Little Grandma	Destiny Starr Lion Shows	62
At Midnight	Curtis D. Yellow Tail	63
Answered Prayers	Tanya Keene	64
There Is No They, Only Us	Monique White Butterfly	67

Drunken Demon That I Wrestle With	*Brandan T.N. McCarty*	68
Not ndn enough	*Carmela Thompson Jr.*	69
Traveling During Summer	*Phillip A. Snow*	71
Dear Brother	*Dominique Johnson*	72
Ex-Con	*Joshua P. Klemm*	75
My Favorite Runner	*Thomas M. Yeahpau*	76
I Am Native American	*Ramona Billy*	85
Old Crow Warriors	*Frederick M. Howe III*	86
Oral Tradition	*Thomas M. Yeahpau*	87
You Stole My Words	*Vena A-dae*	90
Disease	*T. Marie Hart*	91
65-Adam	*Nathaniel Bordeaux*	92
Why the Indians Never Won	*Mary Redhouse*	94
We Finally Won	*Mary Redhouse*	95
For the Children	*Vena A-dae*	97
In the Nicotine Kitchen	*Jennifer Morningstar*	99
That Night	*Desiree Garcia*	100
Within Yourself	*Desiree Garcia*	100
Deep Inside	*Desiree Garcia*	101
This Is Part of Me I Hate	*Brandan T.N. McCarty*	102
Home	*Nicolette E. Kurip*	103

foundry   Shannah Anderson   104

Holding On to the Past   Clarence D. Meat, Jr.   106

I Wonder   Hillary Reed   109

Big Foot   Vincent F. White   110

Eeling   Johnny W. Erickson   112

My Love   Byron "Dirk" Little Light   113

Indian Ballers   Larris Dayne Male Bear   114

Tough Style Rez   Sharla Florez   115

Next Generations   Marcia Blacksmith   116

Woman   Sarah Jerabek   118

When   Destiny Starr Lion Shows   119

When We Are Gone   Angela Damron   120

My Friend   Joshua P. Klemm   121

What Dreams May Come   Jody Roach   122

Living in Two Worlds   Jessie Little Finger   124

"i've been flying my whole life, . . ."   Sunny Rasmussen   125

Window of Dreams   Tellie Parker   126

Giving All I Got   Shane Bruguier   127

Solitary   Tara J. Reel   132

Acknowledgments   135

Editor biographies   144

Preface

The poems and stories collected within this anthology provide a clear vision of how young Indian writers are interpreting and reflecting upon their lives in small towns, reservations, and large metropolitan cities throughout North America. Some of the writers are in college, while many have yet to travel very far from their place of birth. When I became involved in this project, I wanted to assure that the words and visions of these writers remained their own.

As I reread each piece, I can still see the faces of my students, friends, and cousins. I hear the laughter in schoolrooms and the whispering along the roads to where I stand now. Each writer has a unique face and voice, and each stands on ground I can recall.

Annette Piña Ochoa

Introduction

White Lewis A-dae Williams LaBarge Pease White Owl Ortiz Saunooke Brown Redhouse Howe Crazy Mule Snow Frank-Green Moser Damron Joaquin Little Light Yeahpau Bradley Roach Almendarez Pemma Male Bear Perry Left Hand Brien Manriquez McCarty Bright Wings Wild. All these names and more.

Assiniboine Little Shell Chippewa Gros-Ventre Tohono O'odham, Akimel O'odham Kiowa Cochiti Muckleshoot Yakama Umatilla Puyallup Lac du Flambeau Band of Lake Superior Chippewa Little Pine Band of Cree Crow Mandan Hidatsa Acoma Pueblo Eastern Band Cherokee Mohegan Pyramid Lake Paiute Navajo Blackfeet Northern Cheyenne Pomo Yurok Iroquois. All these tribes and more.

Native American people and their tribal communities and cultures go on and on — in a sense, more than we realize. They are stronger and more present than ever. Yes. In fact, more than we realize. This land now called America — including North, Central, and South America — is home to the people and cultures indigenous to the land. The names above are only a small indication of the hold that Indigenous American people have on the present day world. When we hear "we are here" spoken unequivocally in the poetry and stories in *Night Is Gone, Day Is Still Coming,* we realize it is a hold that is forever. And we have to agree that "we are here" is an affirmation and assertion of Indigenous America.

Years ago when I was younger, I often felt I had no ground on which to stand and speak. Even though our Acoma elders constantly encouraged belief and pride in our people's heritage and identity, often their advice and counsel didn't seem to be enough. Hundreds of years of colonization and the harsh historical experiences that our Indigenous peoples had endured affected us severely and traumatically. Even now, in fleeting moments, I sometimes feel that way. However when I see, hear, and read poetry and stories by Native youth speaking strongly, wonderfully, and honestly about land, culture, community, I cannot help but feel the hope and courage with which they sing, dance, shout, and speak.

SIMON J. ORTIZ

Whispers

Have you ever heard a whisper,
calm, gentle, or loud as a freight train?
If you were to whistle in the wind,
would it carry your story?

Let us smudge to purify our whispers, prayers,
and the bread we eat.
Much like the fire smoke carrying the
sweet smell of grease bread,
there is a tender society of young people,
trying to carry out the wisdom of the past.

Their whispers have the fragrance of grease bread.
Even after the smudge is gone,
the performance of life in a young person's mind
records the soft whispers of the heart.

But are the young people's whispers heard?
Though the freight trains are loud and annoying,
some are heard, but many are not.
Though the freight trains are loud and annoying,
push on against the wind.

Who are the ones who never stop to listen?
Who are the ones who operate the loudest
and most annoying machines?
Why does the annoying machine rip through
all the whispers of the young society?

VINCENT F. WHITE, age 20
Assiniboine, Little Shell Chippewa, Banic, Cree, Gros-Ventre

Summertime

It was summer and
I remember taking long
drinks of Coca-Cola that
Grandpa gave me.

Refreshing drinks of
sweet carbonation
and it was good.
Good like redemption.

In the sunlight he
looked like he could
have been a great chief.
In the old days.

It was not his preferred
drink
but he shared the good stuff
with me.

We could finish with
that same ahhhh that
sounded like the greatest
sound ever heard.

Down to the ground the shiny
red cans would fall
and the look of satisfaction and
accomplishment shone in our faces.

Beneath our feet the cans
crumbled.
The way we crushed cans
seemed like an art.
inside. crushed. outside. folded.

It was like a ceremonious
dance, our ritual like the
breaking of the
bread.

As the song ended to our carbonation dance
we both looked at each other.
Without saying a word
we knew it was time.

The bags filled and tied
all the memories sealed
and thirst quenched, it was off
to the city . . .

to trade for more memories.

PATRICK LEWIS, age 16
Tohono O'odham, Akimel O'odham

Subway Mourning

The subway shook
  Annoyed by the weight within its hollowed skin.
The people moved
  Eyes heavy
  Sight pulled to the stained floor
Not speaking

Believing the world is so small
  Breathing the same thick, suffocating New York Air
    Beautiful thought.
Different in the same environment
  Living, standing next to one another.

I am used to being the same
  Same dark skin
  Same choppy accent
  Same word for *grandma*
  Same 50,000 acres space called Cochiti Indian Reservation.

Now in some 20 by 8 square
Squirming beneath the largest city on earth
I am the Cochiti carrot in the huge ethnic salad,
Swallowed by the red 1 and 3 subway going downtown.

Not looking up, I see the old Chinese woman
With a shopping bag filled with clothes,
The old black man,
  Staring at some half-graffitied advertisement.
The tired businessman with a half-wrinkled power tie
  And heavy, brown-leathered briefcase.

Me, the rez girl,
   Without her people,
Cut off by the umbilical cord, told, "Grow up,"
   With an opportunity not given to all rez kids.

Grown-up now.
   Always missing home.

VENA A-DAE, age 19
Kiowa, Cochiti

Red Light. Green Light.

She wakes up in the morning to cars honking.

Bundled up traffic. Pedestrians screaming because
The Yellow Taxi nipped the tips of their shoes.

"Walk" shines the man with no face
Then instantly flashes the Devil's red hand.
No in-between.   Just stop and go.

She watches the businesswomen strutting their
Armani business suits and Clinique painted lips,
Their walk like a runway model without the turns.

Hey! NDN GIRL. FEED ME. FEED ME. PLEASE —
Her stomach pounds at her insides, like a baby reaching out
To the unknown world.
Pounding.   Reaching.   Screaming.
Feed Me.   **Feed Me.**   **Feed ME.**

She stands.   Stretches the kinks out of her neck.
She leaves her velvet black blanket on her paperboard mansion,
And leaves her silver tin pillow
For her neighbor,
A sleeping child,
Who dreams of marbles and G.I. Joe.

She has her VIP pass for the alleys,
Which only the street wanderers
Can obtain. She has a blue sticker on it, which reads:
VIP for the month of October.

Priority Meal Ticket.

She finds a half-eaten jelly doughnut and some orange
Juice left behind Dunkin' Donuts
And indulges in the raspberry jelly
As it greets the tip of her nose.

She walks to a women's day shelter
Five blocks down the street.

She walks.　　She stops.
Red Light.　　Green Light.

GERRI LILLIAN WILLIAMS, age 21
Muckleshoot, Yakama, Umatilla, and Puyallup

My heart was pounding when I sat down on that big hairy animal. I was so scared. Finally the gate flew open and I held on for my life. It was weird, it was like I was on a carnival ride. The wind was blowing in my face. I didn't really see anything 'cause my head was flying everywhere. That was the longest eight seconds of my life. Then I felt my body fall and I tasted dirt as my face hit the ground. I was so relieved that I was safe on the ground. That was the first time I ever rode a steer in a rodeo.

I remember the day when my Uncle Larry first asked me if I wanted to ride steers in the rodeo. I was at my grandma's house one day chillin', when Uncle Larry, who was once a bull rider, was there visiting. He owned cattle and was doing roundup. My uncle asked me and my three younger cousins if we were interested. So I thought about it a lot and went home and told my parents. My mom was scared for me but my dad wanted me to do it. So I let my uncle know I wanted to.

Uncle Larry put my youngest cousin, Raven, who was about five or six, into mutton busting (sheep riding). Then he put me and my two other cousins into steer riding. He told us what to do and how to ride. It was basically holding on as long as you could. We really weren't given any practice, just words of wisdom. He told us how to hold on, where to put our feet, and when to get off if we didn't get bucked off first.

Then the day of my first ride came. Really, I thought it was going to be a piece of cake. But it wasn't as easy as it looked. I was nervous when I saw all those animals staring at me as I stretched and got ready for my turn. It made me nervous that my cousin Alvia and I were the only two girls riding steers.

Eagle and I continued steer riding, and my little cousin Raven continued sheep riding. Alvia, however, didn't like it, so she quit after her first time. As for Eagle, he quit, too, after a while. My cousin Raven stayed in sheep riding for a long while and even won a few times. She liked it a lot. I kept riding steer for a little while longer and finally quit. But I'll never forget that first time. It was scary, but it was also very exciting.

DENISE MARIE JOAQUIN, age 16
Tohono O'odham

Showing Me

The guitar shop
On 30th Street
Where you first
Played me the cords
Showed me how to grip
My own notes
To chase away
Those times I felt less than myself
  The homesickness
    The arguments with my mom
      The loneliness
Eventually you brought me
"Cortez, The Killer"
Muddy Waters
  I know my little baby
  Don't know the shape I'm in
  I ain't had no good lovin'
  Since God knows when
John Lee Hooker
  Don't look back, baby
  Don't look back
Billie Holiday
In my walls
Vibrating in my tears
  Counseling me in slow motion with
  Deliberate poetry put to the guitar
  To make me whole again

You said
You always wanted to give me
What no one else would
Materializing my blues
Into shine on my skin
And life on the tips of
My fingertips

VENA A-DAE, age 18
Kiowa, Cochiti

Camouflage

Since the casino came to town, my last name, my family tree, my heritage have all become questionable. "You've got blue eyes. Your hair isn't black. Is Saunooke Polish?" I hear these questions a lot.

I never asked to be born where I was, but I'm lucky. I get to see how other races really feel about American Indians without the restraint of political correctness. I can't count how many times peers make racist comments without realizing they are offending me. I used to lead two separate lives, but those lives were so conflicting. I now refuse to keep quiet when the football captain calls his teammate a "drunken Indian" and then pats him on the back for winning the game. And I absolutely refuse to embrace silence when a girlfriend accuses another of "only dating Indians." What is that supposed to mean?

It is almost comical to see their startled reactions when I confront them. Their eyes stretch, showing more white than color. Their mouths sag low, grasping for apologetic words in the tense, thick air. And there appear, always, those tiny beads of sweat that collect across their foreheads in an attempt to cool their embarrassment. They stumble over words and ultimately make an attempt to justify ignorance. But I can't blame them. I've met their families. These children are mere scraps cut from the hateful quilts of their parents.

Sometimes I wish I were darker, but then I wouldn't be able to see the truth of both cultures. My skin is a camouflage and my eyes, though blue, are magnifying glasses of a stereotype — a stereotype marked by a little Indian doll with a Hollywood history. Would anyone ever pick out this little Indian doll for Christmas? I doubt it. She's not wearing a pink, silky dress and she doesn't have bleached blond hair. And she certainly doesn't come with a convertible.

But how do you sell a little Indian girl? Easy. Instead of sexy Barbie, she becomes a hopeless orphan of society. She wears her "Native" dress of polyester fringe and lacy bows and her eyes are naturally pink and purple-rimmed. Her lips are genetically stained pink. Sure! Didn't you know that the early Natives always wore their hair in curly pigtails? And her little pug nose is so realistic!

But there stands some truth to her. Over the years, signs of gray have crept in amid the midnight locks of stereotyping. She's a doll but she's had struggle. Imagine how she's had to worry about being the last doll on the shelf at Christmastime. And there's truth in the small speck of blue on her right plastic arm. It's her scar. Everyone has scars. This might be from that time Susie slammed her into the toy box after she tried to steal Ken away from Barbie.

I wonder why we always see these dolls alone. They never travel in herds like other dolls. They don't come with predestined families. They don't own dream houses. But they are here to amuse tourists. And, oh, how they do! These dolls portray cuteness but never strength.

This little Indian doll is one among many. You can see how she's cut from a pattern because the plastic still dangles off her arms and legs. She has lost her individuality.

When faced with the images of society, we are ultimately faced with the truth of its ideals.

ANNETTE BIRD SAUNOOKE, age 18
Eastern Band Cherokee

Disneyland

I tap on the shoulder of
a middle-aged white man
sitting next to me in the whirlpool
at the Crowne Plaza hotel.

Just as the rolling of the whirlpool's jets ceases
stillness
enters
so we may consider each other

first time
last time

I thought California was my kinda place to be.

so I just had to ask:

Can you tell me where I left my world?
(because I thought he might know)

I swear I left it right here next to your tube of SPF 80 sunscreen.
Aren't the stars pretty?
(because they were, and I thought he might agree)

I only stepped away for a second. . . .

His blue trunks drip as he walks to the whirlpool's dial.

Nice middle-aged white man's son emerges from the shallow
  end of the pool
chlorinated transparent blue under an orange Anaheim sky
and asks:

"Daddy, can we sit in the hot pool for a while?
Please, Daddy?"

"No, son."

"Please, Daddy?"
A pink toe touches the still tub's warm aqua liquid.

"No! Eric, we've talked about this."

"I'm sorry, miss.
I don't know what to tell you.
It was just working a minute ago. . . ."

I'm sorry what did you say?

faintly . . .

It's okay.

All I see is pale wet backs
shining under fogged California moonlight
as
the
man and his son
walk
away

SARA M. ORTIZ, age 18
Acoma Pueblo

The Dance

I see outlines of trees, standing with their strong roots shadowed by the black night, and the stars that pierce the sky with their brightness.

By the outside fire, all male dancers prepare themselves for the dance. We strip down to only our shorts, then carefully put on our necklaces made of shells, nuts, and bear grass.

A man hands us a branch of brush. I clench it in my right hand, as my body fills with pride, thinking of the people who have held this piece before me.

Another man hands me a mink-skin pouch that is full of arrows. He then goes to a shed and brings hands full of head-bands and feathers. We put on our head-bands and put the feathers in place.

It is now time to line up and start our journey to the hole. How honored I am to walk the very trail that my ancestors have walked before me, and that my children and grandchildren will walk for generations to come.

Only the shapes of our bodies can be seen coming in the sacred night. We start walking down the hill and the mighty wind comes, making the fire open its mouth, letting out its magical sparks. The sparks light up the faces of the medicine woman, a sick child, and his mother. In front of me a young boy follows his grandfather. I think to myself how lucky this young boy is to share this moment with him.

Now in the hole, I cannot see any of the faces above, but I know that the elders are watching, clenching their blankets to protect them from the cool ocean winds at the mouth of the Klamath River.

We pray for healing, dancing in a square counterclockwise, singing in our native tongue. Leaves fall and are carried away by the wind, sending a chill of mythical excitement up my back. It is then that I look up and see the brightest star twinkle in the darkness. It is My Grandfather winking down at me from the heavens, telling me, "Good Job, Frankie. I am proud of you."

I, too, am a lucky boy.

Skylar Frank-Green Moser, age 13
Yurok

Red Girls

There are such girls as red girls
They walk with pride in themselves
They love warriors
They play ball
They are the child-bearers
They are our mothers
They are the food-makers
They are red girls
They are strong and beautiful
With their red flawless skin
The girls of these beautiful women
Are so strong and can do everything
The warriors love them and adore them
They take care of them.
They are Native Americans and proud
The red girls.

MARY REDHOUSE, age 16
Pyramid Lake Paiute, Walker River Paiute, Wind Rock Navajo

The Crow Fair of Yesteryear

Hookie-bobbing
and cop-dodging,
running back to camp.
Quick, grab the lamp.

Time to wake, watch the parade,
sit and watch in the cool shade.
This time should never fade.

They're having a rodeo today.
Get some money, we might have to pay.
Or, let's just sneak in,
go around back and mess with the bulls
 in the pen.

FREDERICK M. HOWE III, age 17
Crow, Blackfeet

Handsome Indian Boy

As I was walking around the arbor,
I saw a handsome Indian boy
Dancing around in his shiny outfit —
Just dancing fast, hoping to win —
A handsome Indian boy,
Just looking fine and
Dancing in the wind
Till the drum stops.
He stops. He looks.
I look. He's just the most handsome boy
I've ever seen.

JOANNA M. CRAZY MULE, age 15
Crow, Northern Cheyenne

Berry Paints

Plump,
Ripe,
Round.
Hanging,
Dangling,
Down.
Squish,
Squash,
Squirt.
Dip,
Stroke.
Dip,
Stroke.
Vivid
Canvas
of Colors

MIKEL D. BROWN, age 13
The Mohegan Tribe of Connecticut

Who Am I?

Who am I?
Am I the person of my past
Am I the person who is lost

Who am I?
I hear tales of my ancestors
I feel my chest fill with pride
Knowing where I am from

But . . .
I can never live as they did
So my past is my past

Who am I?
I search for an identity
I look to my television
I find gangster-rap stars
And Latin gangs
Catch my eye

But . . .
I am proud of my past
And where I come from
So I put those ideas to the side
And I again wonder

Who am I?
When I have tried to be traditional
People not only in their words
But in their looks say to me
"Just who do you think you're trying to be!"
These words and looks rip through my soul
And make me feel like I was stabbed
Many times with a double-edged knife
All I can do is wonder

Who am I?

ROGER D. WHITE OWL, age 22
Mandan, Hidatsa

The Gap

A wise, old drunkard once told me about a meeting place
  a meeting place called the Gap.
He told me this place existed between our world
  and the civilized one.
There were no laws, no elders to tell you what to do
  Indians could be as free as ever.
He told me at night when the wind blew hard
  and ran through the glowing red-rock cliffs.

The wind would sing an old "49" song and the Kiowas
  would join in:

> *Indian — girls*
> *Indian — girls*
> *Oh, how I love them Indian girls*

I thought, *What a crazy old man,* and shouted,
  "He deserves a beer!" as everyone in the circle laughed.
I wish I had a nickel for every beer consumed at the Gap
  No Indian would ever have to work again.
I know why people come here, not just to socialize, fight, or
  snag but to hide from their responsibilities and problems.
I stood there last, sharing old memories of true friends, who are
  dead while making new memories with friends still living.
Then the wind started singing a "49" song and the Kiowas
  joined in:

> *She got mad at me*
> *'Cause she caught me*
> *Talking to my old-timer*

As I relieved myself, I stared at the Gap's ditch and the many
   colors: anger, happiness, stress, congrats, and
   long time no see.
Walking across the rock-colored road, a car full of rugged
   Indian babes pulled over. "Come on, get in, let's go!"
As I sat in the backseat, I asked, "Where are we going?"
   "We're taking you home."
"Wah, I was just at home, you're taking me back to the civilized
   world, let me out."
As I walked back up the hill to the Gap, I felt the wind
   behind me.

The wind started to sing a new "49" song and I joined in:
   Damn, my honey left me
   It's okay, it's all right
   'Cause my new one cooks me fry bread every night.
   Hay-ya, hay-ya, hay-ya

THOMAS M. YEAHPAU, age 21
Kiowa

My Mind's Words

Time after time I sit and think about things gone wrong
How am I holding on?
I've got to be strong
I sit and whisper memories of the future
That time has yet to pass
In this race against time
I will always end up in last
Is the answer out there?
Is the answer in me?
You know the answer, but why can't I see?
If it were my choice I would never die
I would live on
It's not my choice, so it's a matter of time til I'm gone
Inside my mind is where I am free
I know god personally
Sometimes I call him me
Go 'head pull that gun out and see what a bullet does
Let's worry about right now and not about what was

A pen and paper
Notebook under light
Thoughts made into words
Think and start to write
Know your friends from your enemies
Sometimes your friends are your enemies
They just have secret identities
Undercover, ready to stab you in the back unexpected
An honest friendship shattered and I wrecked it
I still exist

You can't scare me out of my world
Life is something I can't resist
Every day I'm scared, but I'm not afraid
My life is dark
Life in the shade
Happy days of summer
Miseries of winter
Emotion is a season
I am a basket case, but I am very sane and I have my reason
Like a game of chess I plan my attack to get one step ahead
Checkmate, I'm held back
I live life, but life is dead
Fly free, just like the birds
My mind's free and these are my mind's words

JORELL "SPACE MAN" X. LABARGE, age 14
Lac du Flambeau Band of Lake Superior Chippewa

Butch's Drop

My younger brother Butch was my sidekick growing up. We were forced to do everything together and we made the most of it. I actually liked him around, even though I beat his ass most of the time, because he gave me someone to blame my wrongdoings on. He was also my guinea pig. An example of this was when we were kids, sometimes I would talk him into holding different fireworks in his hand while they exploded, just so he could tell me which ones hurt the most. I was really good at making it sound like it was a cool thing to do. He always looked up to me in those days, poor guy. That brings me to the story of Butch's drop, because it's the story of how Butch got everybody our age in our area to look up to him, myself included.

When I was ten and Butch was eight, we were into riding bikes and everything that goes with it. We were just two average, little Indian boys, with bowl haircuts, knee-high socks, and a lot of free time. Every kid, at that time, had a bike in Anadarko, Oklahoma, even if they were from poor families that couldn't afford luxuries. The kids from poor families, like Butch and me, had bikes with different parts on them. We would ride on bikes with Mongoose handlebars, a Diamondback frame, and Sigma wheels. They were mix-matched because they were bikes that we put together with the twenty or so bikes we stole. In order to not get caught on a stolen bike, we had to mix-match them. Every day we rode them bikes, like some kind of Hell's Angels youth group, and hung out at stores, houses, and trails doing tricks. They were precious times for us, as we rode in the wind, like Indian kids carelessly rode ponies in the old days. There were bike routes and shortcuts to everywhere that we used, but there was this one place that threw off our whole system because it blocked us off. It was an irrigation ditch, between Mississippi Street and Colorado Street, which was about fifteen feet wide and ten feet deep and not paved, like them fancy-neighborhood irrigation ditches. Not only was it not paved, but it was so rocky from a failed attempt to pave it that it made it almost impossible to walk our bikes down and up it. Every time we got to this area, it delayed us and the bad thing was, it went right through our neighborhood. We had to go two blocks either way to get around it, and when you're that young, two blocks is a long way.

My friends and I sat at the edge of this ditch one day, trying to figure out a way to cross it without having to build a bridge, because we had built bridges before, and the teenagers always knocked them over. Then out of nowhere, I came up with a master plan. I recommended that we build two ramps to jump over it, but that we tie a rope on the back of each one. When you were ready, you could use the rope to pull the ramp out of the ditch, throw the rope to the other side, and jump the ditch. Once across, you could pull the ramp back into the ditch and toss the rope back to the other side for the next person's use. This would prevent teenagers from messing with our ramps, and we would have one for each side. Everybody liked the plan and we built the two ramps that afternoon. They were not your average ramps either; they were awesome daredevil ramps. Next, we had to find someone to test out our brilliant plan. No one volunteered, but I remembered a comment Butch had made about how he wished he could jump the ramps we were building. I told my crew I would have Butch over the next day to make the daring jump and I invited everyone I knew to witness it. All I had to do was sweet-talk Butch.

That same evening, I went home and found Butch playing with my Transformers. I usually would have made him cry for such a crime, but not that day. Not only did I let him play with them, I joined in with him. He was so happy, I knew he was vulnerable. The mouse took the cheese. In a concerned tone, I asked him if he remembered the ramps I was building and he told me he did. After giving him a "no I shouldn't" look, I asked if he wanted to jump one, and he accepted the offer without hesitation. Then I asked if he wanted to jump over the ditch where we had the ramps. He was a little curious about why I didn't want to do it, but I convinced him that it was too easy for me, and I thought I would give him an opportunity to get some props in our neighborhood. My lie made him even more willing to give it a try. Now, I would never send Butch on a kamikaze journey, so we rode to the ditch and I let him try the ramps a couple of times in the street. He proved himself a good rider; hell, he learned from one of the best, me. We went back home to our house and I wished him good luck before we went to sleep. His eyes were gleaming with excitement.

The next day was a Saturday, and every kid in our town had heard about Butch's upcoming stunt. Kids from every neighborhood, rich and poor, were there to greet Butch and me. When we arrived, he asked me why there was such a crowd, and I convinced him it was a great occasion that we finally found a way around that ditch. I knew Butch was nervous, so I gave him a pep talk, telling him he could do anything he put his mind to and not to pay attention to all the people, to just picture me and him as the only ones there. After listening to one of my greatest speeches, he had a look that said he could do anything. Butch was a soldier going to the front line in a battle. I let him use my bike, even though I knew I might not ever see it again. I think it was the only time he ever touched my bike without getting a severe beating for it. He got on, with no fear, and warmed up a little, as the crowd built on both sides of the ugliest ditch in the world. There were even older people there, who had just walked by and heard what Butch was about to attempt.

Butch stopped a block away from the ramp and viewed his destiny. Everybody asked themselves, "Is he going to do it?" Then all of a sudden, Butch took off like the space shuttle Challenger. He built speed with each foot he traveled and everybody tensed up when he passed the crowd, but right when he hit the ramp, he braked. Stopping at the fast speed he was going caused him to skid all the way up the ramp and almost shoot off anyway. Everybody "awed" in disappointment, so I ran to him to see what was up. He said he felt he could've built more speed if he started even farther away, so I told him to go for it. I calmed the crowd down by explaining his decision, like they paid for the show, and Butch rode off to his new starting spot, which was a block and a half away. Butch shot off like a rocket again, and this time even faster. He was going so fast that he was just a blur when he reached us. At the speed he hit the ramp, everybody knew he couldn't turn back and the tension was so thick in the air, no one could move. Like a sign from God, believed only by the witnesses, he shot off the ramp in a "cannonball-out-of-a-cannon" fashion. Everybody's mouths were wide open in disbelief. I looked in the air and couldn't believe my brother was doing it.

For two seconds, he grew wings and turned into an eagle.
    He flew over everybody's teepee and gave out a war cry.
For two seconds, our ancestors stood on their graves and sang a
    victory song. It was the one about the mouse that outsmarted
    the wolf.
For two seconds, anybody could do anything. He made nothing
    impossible and that was what he taught everybody watching
    him.
For two seconds, he turned into the Greek god Helios, but
    instead of riding a chariot across the sky, he rode a bike.
For two seconds, my brother tried to prove Newton's laws of
    gravity wrong. "What goes up don't always have to come down,"
    my brother said and tried to prove.
For two seconds, my brother was the Indian Evel Knievel.
    He was the Indian Michael "Air" Jordan. He was our hero.
For two seconds, I saw my brother the happiest I've ever seen
    him, and I knew he didn't want to come down. I told him to
    fly to heaven and tell grandma I said, "Hello."

Then the third second hit and I remembered something I should've told my brother. I forgot to tell him my pony was wounded. My pony's neck was weak and stripped, which caused the handlebars to slip back and forth after hard jolts. I tried to yell over the cheering crowd, but it was no use. The fourth second hit and the front wheel of the bike hit the ground on the other side. Just as the back wheel landed, the shit hit the fan. The landing was rough and it caused the handlebars to bend all the way forward, with my brother still holding on. Butch busted his chin on the neck of the frame, and the wheel turned sideways, causing the bike to flip. He went over with the bike and rolled it a couple of times, tangling himself in it. As fast as I could, I ran down and up the ditch to his side and tore my bike away from his body. His body was limp as I picked up his head and told him to speak to me. After looking around in a daze, he asked if it was really me. I told him it was and that everything was going to be all right. In a soft, battered voice, he asked if he made it, and I told him he did and how beautiful it was. He coughed and told me to tell his kids about it. After that, he pretended to die, and I yelled out, "Why!"

Since then, I have never heard of anybody else attempting to jump the ditch. I know none of us did, especially after we saw Butch's courageous leap. They call the spot where he jumped "Butch's Drop," even though he didn't die. Kids still sit there on bikes and try to figure out ways across Butch's Drop without going out the way he did. Every now and then, I ask my grown brother to do it again, but he just smiles at me.

Thomas M. Yeahpau, age 20
Kiowa

Pouring Milk Before Cereal

For My Uncle Pee-Wee

He poured his milk
  Before his cereal
Because we needed the calcium.

Globe-size Kiowa guy, 6'3"
  Combing the knots
Out of my little brother's hair

Washing away the stale smell
  Of Budweiser
And sight of lanky Corona bottles

While chasing away the hunger
  Clinging to the
Inner lining of our tummies

With the softness of his voice
  Like fine red dust
Piled around Hog Creek, Oklahoma.

We all had big bones, big feet, big noses
  Handed down from
Fierce Kiowa warriors.

The war has changed
  To battles with
Alcoholism and diabetes and heartsickness.

To him, it was just a matter of nutrition
  That began with

Breakfast, the most important meal of our lives.

Uncle Pee-Wee, Urban Kiowa
  Said we'd be just fine
Because he poured his milk before his cereal.

VENA A-DAE, age 17
Kiowa, Cochiti

≋ ≋ ≋

I remember the Vodka Summer when I was only eleven. My sixteen-year-old sister left me alone to raise two boys we called brothers while she drank my aunt's bitter water in beautiful bottles. I struggled to learn how to make fried eggs so the brothers would not starve. I aged twenty years in one summer and I haven't seen my childhood since.

That summer I listened at the bathroom door to the lurching of my sister's stomach. I secretly denied the heredity of alcoholism in my genes — braided, twisted, entwined, fused into my DNA. I cried, hoping it would drip away with my tears. Drip into the clothes I wore and be washed out in the laundry. The alcohol stained my sister's womb and you can still smell the liquor on her son's breath.

Today as I watched her coolly twist open another bottle, I noticed it was the same color as her eyes. Beer-bottle eyes. I almost laughed to myself. I almost cried out loud. As she stood there and so unladylike gulped down a bottle of self-destruction. I wanted to slink away and find a mirror. Just so I could make sure my eyes were still the deep green they were when I woke up this morning and everyone was sober.

Shattering my thoughts, a bottle of cold apple wine is slipped into my hands. The smooth glass reminds me of the roughness of my own palms. Rough with over forty years crammed into my eighteen-year-old body. I feel the cold glass of that cheap bottle of wine and deep inside I cry. I cry for all those who were handed the same legacy, and died trying to keep it alive. Maybe I will die before it does, but it will never kill me. . . .

I can feel the explosion of glass and cheap wine on the hot asphalt release me from a five-hundred-year-old burden.

NAKESHA BRADLEY, age 18
Eastern Cherokee

Her blood runs proud with her heritage.
To her customs she holds true.
She walks our land with dignity,
In spite of the red, white, and blue.

Attacks on her people are frequent.
Respect! She'll stand for no less.
She gives, yet doesn't like receiving.
Loving is what she does best.

She'll stand when everyone is sitting.
Afraid to speak truth, she is not.
She fights for the rights and traditions
Her ancestors forever sought.

But now old age is ensuing. . . .
She must fight for her life, her alone.
And I stand by her side until death.
In her struggle, I find my own.

My grandmother is my true friend.
She is the woman I strive to be.
I'd give up my life for her instantly,
Though I know she'd never let me.

I don't have much to give this woman
Who has spent all her life being strong.
All I can do is carry her name
And hope that *our* fight doesn't last long.

I will fight for the rights she demanded,
For our people, our native tribe.
I will do as my soulmate wants;
I will keep the spirit alive.

I will learn to live without the one I love most.
In Little Red Bird, Red Feather will live.

CARRIE M. BROWN — "Squayojeetsesh (Little Red Bird)," age 18
Mohegan Tribe

Untitled '96

Who knows what it is like to fly away?
the ladies in the back sucking on corn for luck

There are wings in the backs of the old ones
protecting fresh eyes from dust and harm,
waking with cobwebbed hearts and yellow tears
we feed the corn our dead

Memories of dance
come for their own . . . special space
we are the creatures
we are beings
changing for balance
changing for song

We are the freedom who chooses life without veil
carrying burdens
to lay the baskets down
to lay down the pipes of dreams

I hear a song now
a stream of endless voices
birds of fashion fall away
flute music player
your whisp has caught my ear

Angela, age 19
Cherokee, Iroquois

Butterfly Princess

In the morning I had to climb the rainbow mounds in the laundry room. It was the day of the awards assembly. I thought I might get an award. I wanted to make my mother proud.

I accidentally knocked over the Tide box, and it fell over the clothes like magic fairy dust sprinkled by a pretty little fairy with lavender and silver wings. I was digging through the pot of gold, and I found my gray jeans, which used to be black, and my Rainbow Brite T-shirt. My jeans hugged my little thighs and reached below my knobby knees. My T-shirt only reached my bellybutton. It was my mother's favorite. Whenever I wore it, she said I looked like a butterfly princess.

I parted my uneven hair down the middle,
And I brushed my crooked teeth with
Bubble gum toothpaste.
"I'm going to school now, mommy,"
I whispered to her in her dreams.
She was passed out on the sofa stained brown with
Folgers and Sockeye.
No one else was home — just my mom, and the nauseating
    waves flying backward
full of Chinook and Coho, 100 Lights and Camels.
I walked three blocks down the road, dragging my right foot to
    keep my leather shoe on.
My left shoe was still stitched, but the corner of my right shoe
    was torn.
On the blacktop, all the students were still standing in line
    outside of the classrooms.
    "I could easily tip them over,
        And they would fall like dominoes,"
        I thought to myself.

I strolled past the sixth-graders. Then the fifth-graders.
A fourth-grader with freckles and wide cheeks chuckled,
   "Look at her! The Freak! She doesn't know how to walk!"

I kept dragging my right foot across the endless blacktop,
I created the Green River, as it followed me
Past the laughing coyotes on the basketball court,
Past the fourth-graders,
And then relieved, into
My classroom.
   I dragged my right foot to the coat rack
      And hung up my Pendleton jacket.
Tap. Tap.
I turned around and saw the new girl from New York.
Her name is Shayla, and she has real dark skin.
"I thought you might like my gym shoes. My mommy said I
   could give them to you. Here."
I reached out and grabbed them. I put them on quickly.
I hadn't gotten a new pair of shoes since second grade.
"They will match your shirt. Rainbow Brite is my favorite, too."
Shayla smiled and walked to her desk.

"Okay, class. Hurry up. Get in line. We have an awards assembly
   today,"
Mrs. Johnson said through metallic eyes.
We all lined up at the water fountain.
Shayla
stood right behind me.

The line jumped and bounced around like Tigger all the way to
   the gym.

· · ·

"I love your new shoes," Mrs. Johnson told me.
The butterflies on my shirt fluttered away,
And one landed on Shayla's hand.
We both giggled.

The awards were given to the first- and second-graders.
It was **finally** time for the third-graders' awards.
The kindness award for Mrs. Johnson's class goes to: **Shayla!**

I clapped as Shayla ran up to get her award.
The purple and green butterflies fluttered right behind her.
Her smile ran to the Bronx and back.

Then she ran back to our class row.
When she sat down, she tore her award in half. She kept the part
  with her name on it,
And on the other half
She wrote my name in green crayon.
My crooked teeth shined.

I ran home after school that day to show my mother the award.
I wanted to show her my new rainbow shoes, too,
But she was still out swimming
  With
    The Chinook.

Gerri Lillian Williams, age 22
Muckleshoot, Yakama, Umatilla, and Puyallup

Susto

If I knew the *curandera* practices
I'd take my mom by the hand

Lead her to the house she's never been,
to my own room. She'd sit on my bed crying soft.

I'd begin the healing
with a bunch of sacred tree branches.

I'd make invisible crosses on every limb
of her body. I'd start with her heart

and while the crosses were traveling
from heart to head, to womb, and back again

I'd whisper urgent prayers
Dios mio cura mi mama. Que no se vaya.

After I'd enveloped her in crosses and prayers
I'd drape a dark towel over her soft hair

And as if playing peek-a-boo with a baby
I'd put my head under the towel close to hers.

As we shared the sweet-smell healing branches
through cupped hands I'd whisper

Adriana, no te vayas, aqui estoy. No te vayas.
And after that she wouldn't go.

Instead of the airport we'd go to the park
and she, smiling, would stay.

But I don't know the healing practices of my ancestors.
All I know is that mama is leaving, again.

I make an invisible cross anyway.
In my father's arms, he restrains legs that would run,

that are running, arms that won't abide, flail until,
exhausted, they stretch like the golden image

next to mama's heart. But the sound of the engine
is too loud for her to hear my prayers.

She goes, doesn't look back.
And my prayers are the same.

AYME ALMENDAREZ, age 20
Mexica Nation

Mom's Fry Bread

Mom's fry bread is the bomb!
If you're upset, take one bite and it'll make you calm.

It smells so *mmm, mmm!*
that you could turn it into a perfume.

Mom's fry bread is all that and a bag of chips
but watch out — too much of it could
enlarge your hips!

The fry bread pan
is *ummm* . . .
more sacred than a temple in Japan!

You can eat Mom's fry bread any season,
it'll warm you up if you're freezing.

During Christmas, people give cookies. . . .
We give bread!
It's so soft it reminds me of my bed.

Mom's fry bread keeps Prancer prancing,
during the summer it keeps me dancing.

The wait for Mom's fry bread is long
but it's worth it, when your mom's fry bread
is the Bomb!

LATEACHIA PEMMA, age 17
Forest County Potawatomi

My Indian Pooh Bear

My Indian pooh bear is skinny, hungry, and brown.
My Indian pooh bear does not eat honey.
My Indian pooh bear eats fry bread with honey.
My Indian pooh bear does not sing "Hungry in My Tummy."
My Indian pooh bear sings forty-nines.
My Indian pooh bear's friend is not Piglet
but old man coyote.
My Indian pooh bear does not know Tigger,
but only knows Red Women.
My Indian pooh bear does not wear a red shirt
but moccasins and buckskins.
My Indian pooh bear does not giggle
but only makes the sounds of the war hoops.
My Indian pooh bear is a Crow.

BETHYANA J. PEASE, age 16
Little Pine Band of Crees in Canada, Crow

Neah Bay, Washington, to Me

Where the ocean lays everywhere, as far as the eye can see.
Almost 360 degrees as well, a great mixture of pine
and cedar trees, and other trees, too, like maple, oak, and ash.
Salt water, pine, cedar, and fires filling my nose
when I step foot out of Mama Jane's van.
A long drive to get to my second home, Neah Bay,
but well worth it.

The rain falling on my face and head as I sit and watch
my Grandpa Pug carve his daily work.
His daily work is model canoes, masks, paddles, and etc.
All painted in traditional colors when done —
red, black, and white.
Grandpa Pug is not doing too well, as I notice visiting him.
He is losing his hearing and has been ill lately —
got the word when I called home
some time ago.

We prepare some fish, not just any fish
but some sockeye or Chinook salmon,
in the day of my return.
We trade stories as well.
The salmon and Ritz or Saltine crackers is like a traditional meal.
Oh, and Grandpa's Root Beer Barrels.
A&W Root Beer Barrels are always on his coffee table.

The moon rises, and his dogs begin to bark.
Time for dinner for the dogs.
::Chuckles:: Grandpa is the carver and the dog man of the tribe.
He is that because he takes all the unwanted dogs under his roof.
This is Neah Bay, Washington, and part of my day back home.
Man, I miss home and wish to return home soon.

BRANDAN T.N. MCCARTY, age 19
Makah

As I Looked

One night I had a dream. I dreamed that I was on a mountain above my village, and as I looked I saw my grandmother very young and alive. She was weaving a basket for her daughter. The basket was a medicine basket for her daughter to dance with. And when she gave it to her daughter, the daughter was unappreciative but took it anyway. I began to look around myself and I saw deep, dark clouds over my head. Everything looked bad. As I continued to look it only got worse. I awoke in the morning and I learned something from my dream. If I don't respect my heritage it will slip away.

KATRINA PERRY, age 11
Hupa

Grandma

Grandma sits and smokes,
listening to the beat of the drum.
She watches as the dancers' feet move
in unison along the grass.
Above, the sun is beating down upon
their faces as the new day arrives.
The day of dancing has come.
Grandma looks up with pride as the
dancers come and form a circle.
There are many dancers in the
circle. She closes her eyes,
trying to remember what it was like
to be a part of that great circle.
Then she looks up, up into
the sky as an eagle soars above them.
She smiles, then she gets a feeling to dance
way down somewhere deep inside. Her legs start
moving with the beat, the singing gets to her
and she sings, bobbing up and down.
Then all of a sudden her heart soars
Like the eagle in the sky.

MELVIN LEFT HAND, age 15
Crow

Would You Cry?

Grandma, would you
cry if you saw us now?
When you left, the air was
fresh and clean,
buffalo roamed and
eagles soared.
Now they're gone.

Grandma, would you
cry if you saw us now?
People don't respect
or care about each other.
We don't pray or listen
like we should.

Grandma, would you cry
if you saw us now?
Can we change and
learn, the way
you taught us to?
Help us, Grandma, if you can.

MARIA LEE FEATHER BRIEN, age 16
Standing Rock Sioux

Dark Waters

When I look
into my grandmother's eyes

I see her standing
in a steam-filled kitchen

making tortillas
for twelve hungry mouths

as rivers of sweat
mixed with tears

fall down her face
when she realizes

she is all alone.

SONIA MANRIQUEZ, age 17
Blackfoot

❦ ❦ ❦

Dear Mother,

I am twenty-two years old now, and I am writing you this letter so that you will understand where I have been in my life. I have been through a lot so far, and you don't even know about half of it. It is time I release these words so I can move forward.

My cousin once told me, "You go to college, write about everything in your life. Write about the good times and the bad. Write so you can release all that pain and anger. Write about the happy times and the lessons you have learned. Write about the life in the ghetto. Get it out of you and move on. Don't ever look back upon the negativity; don't let it bring you down. And once you have done that, you will be free to be yourself. You will be free to live your life the way you choose. Go to college. Get it all out of you. Then you will truly be happy. Then the smile on your face will be of real happiness." Those words stuck with me.

I'll start with the bits and pieces of my childhood. I don't remember my biological father being around. I know you divorced him. It is way disgusting to me to know what he did. How could he molest family members and feel no shame or remorse? Once the reality of those incidents sunk in, I felt sick to my stomach. Way sick. Why would I want to acknowledge my biological father, when he has done this to my family? He's been in and out of prison. He's been in and out of mental institutions. He is a continuous alcoholic. And he's never been a part of my life.

I am happy with my stepfather. He and his children filled my childhood with a lot of great memories. They filled my life with a lot of love. But, I know you and Dad drank a lot. My eldest sister took on the responsibility of being the mom in our family. We were a dysfunctional family, torn apart by alcoholism. But all in all, we managed to get through that part of our lives just fine.

When I was twelve, I was raped. We both know who did that to me. I didn't press charges, because I was beaten up every day for a week, by people from his family. They threatened to kill you and me. I did what I felt was right at the time to protect my family.

Soon after that incident, you quit drinking. Or was it a little bit before that? I don't really remember because by then I was so out of control. I got into a lot of fights at school. I beat up a lot of innocent people. I got kicked out of school all the time. I know it was hard for you to deal with me. You were early in your recovery, and I was too much for you.

I went to live with my cousins on the REZ. It felt as if the whole REZ hated me because no one believed I was really raped by that guy. How could someone from such a good family do such a thing, you know?

We had lived in the city projects, so moving to the REZ was quite a change for me. I had my first taste of alcohol when I lived there. I was with two of my cousins. We walked across the road to the ball field. It was late in the evening and no one was around. One cousin pushed me up against the bathroom stall. The other opened the forty of Olde English 800 and poured it down my throat. I know it sounds ridiculous now, but that was how I started drinking.

Then I got involved with gangs. I had the strength and power to get my own gang established, which I did. I know it drove you crazy, but I had a family within the gangs. I had security. I had the love. I had true friends. They are part of the reason why I am still alive today. The other part is because God has something special planned for me.

I was kicked out of my relatives' house on the reservation and I was on the streets, off and on, for almost a year. I was in and out of juvenile hall and got kicked out of two school districts for truancy, fighting, and gang activity. I became involved with a lot of the Native gangs. They didn't care that I was affiliated with the Crips, because to them, I was just another Native trying to survive. If you were Native and on the streets, they had your back.

A lot of other things happened to me. I'm not going to say when, or by whom, but I want you to know. I was drinking heavily. I was gang-raped. And I witnessed a murder. I almost died twice, but the EMTs were able to revive me, and keep me here. I am grateful to them for my life.

A few times, you came looking for me when I was on the streets. That was something none of my street friends had: a mother out there looking for them. It means a lot to me now, because you were always thinking about me. You were silently expressing your love to me, and my spirit heard it. My spirit felt your love, even when I couldn't.

I remember the day you signed me over to the courts. I know it must have almost killed you to sign papers giving up custody of your baby daughter. But I don't blame you. There was another reason behind all of that. I never would have experienced the life I did, if you hadn't made such choices.

I was placed in a youth home, which provided stability. The youth workers filled my life with love, structure, and guidance. They gave me the space I needed to grow up. They let me learn from my mistakes. They never gave up on **Me.** To this day, the youth workers still love me as their daughter. I was there almost four years, and I wouldn't change any of it. I met a lot of different people there, too. The residents varied in age: from twelve to twenty-one. They all came from different backgrounds: preppy rich kids, gothic street kids, gangsters, gay, lesbian, transgender, Native American, Asian, Mexican, African American, Caucasian, and every other type of person. That alone opened my eyes to a diverse world.

I was first sent to an alcohol treatment center while I lived there. You came with me. I don't remember the trip, but I remember you crying after I was signed in. I started to walk away, then turned to wave goodbye.

I still see the pain in your eyes. In my memories, I want to erase the tears from your eyes, but you needed them to heal your spirit. You saw it as your fault, not mine. But you know what? I needed that experience. I wouldn't be who I am today without it. Things happen in our lives that we have no control over. Things happen for a reason.

After living at my youth home, I went to a boarding school. I accomplished a lot there. I was Associate Student Body President, senior newspaper editor, yearbook editor/producer, involved in our drama club and women's drumming group, a cheerleader, and Homecoming Queen. In the end, I got my GED.

And now I'm in college. I have accepted all the things that happened to me. I worked through the pain and anger. I have come to let go of the past, but not the lessons. I know it is a lot to grasp, especially because this is the first time you are hearing of some of the incidents. But please don't feel bad for me. They no longer have that power or control over me. I am no longer affiliated with the gangs, and I am ready to work toward my future.

I think I was meant to have gone through these painful experiences, because **I AM STRONG ENOUGH TO HANDLE IT.** And now, I am able to help other people who are going through similar experiences and don't know what to do.

One more thing before I close. I want to let you know I appreciate everything you have done for me. I appreciate my Elvis music box. I appreciate the Valentine's Day packages. I appreciate the phone cards you send me and all the times you've spoken to me in your silent words. I appreciate your beauty, Mother, and I love you, and I thank you.

Love always,
Your Daughter

Young at Heart

I am a mother, young at heart.
Yes, I did get pregnant at the age of 17.
Yes, I did have my son, at the age of 18.
Hey, I know this is not normal for girls
to have babies when they are still young ladies!
But, hey, I was strong enough to go through the pain
of others pointing their fingers and laughing at me.
Yes, it was very painful and hard to get up in the morning
knowing that people are thinking you are crazy!
But, hey, I am me.
I am a young mother at heart.

JODY ROACH, age 18
Inuk

Young at Heart

ᐆᒻᒪᑎᒃᑯᑦ ᒪᒃᑯᒃᑐᔪᖕᒐ

ᐋᓈᓇᐅᔪᖕᒐ, ᐆᒻᒪᑎᒃᑯᑦ ᒪᒃᑯᒃᑑᓪᓗᖕᒐ.
ᐄ, ᓯᖕᒐᐃᓂᓚᐅᖅᓯᒪᔪᖕᒐ 17-ᓂᒃ ᐅᑭᐅᕐᑲᑐᐃᓐᓇᖅᓱᖕᒐ
ᐄᓗ, ᐃᕐᓂᖅᑖᓚᐅᖅᓯᒪᔪᖕᒐ ᐅᑭᐅᕐᑲᖅᓱᖕᒐ 18-ᓂᒃ
ᐃᓛᒃ ᑕᒪᓐᓇ ᓈᒻᒪᖕᒥᑦᑑᔪᖅ ᒪᒃᑯᓗᐊᖅᓱᓂ ᓄᑕᕋᖅᑖᕐᑲᑦᑕᕐᓂᖅ
ᑭᓯᐊᓂ, ᐋᓐᓂᕐᓈᓗᒃᑲᓗᐊᖅᑎᓪᓗᒍ ᐱᐊᓂᒍ ᐱᐊᓂᒍᑎᓚᐊᖅᑐᖕᒐ ᐃᓄᖕᓄᑦ
ᑎᒃᑯᐊᖅᑕᐅᓪᓗᖕᒐ ᐊᒻᒪᓗ ᐃᔪᕆᔭᐅᕐᑲᑦᑕᖅᓱᖕᒐ.
ᐃᓛᒃ, ᐋᓐᓂᕐᓇᕐᑲᑦᑕᓚᐅᖅᑐᖅ ᐊᒻᒪᓗ ᐊᒃᓯᕈᕐᓇᖅᓱᓂ ᒪᑭᓐᓇᓯᒃᓱᓂ ᐅᑉᓛᒃᑯᑦ
ᐃᓄᖕᓄᑦ ᓈᒻᒪᒥᔭᐅᖕᒥᔾᓱᓂ.
ᑭᓯᐊᓂ, ᐅᕙᖕᒐᐅᔪᖕᒐ.
ᐅᒻᒪᑕᒃᑯᑦ ᒪᒃᑯᒃᑐᔪᖕᒐ.

ᔩᑎ ᕉᑦᔾ
ᐅᑯᓇᖕᒑᖅᑐᖅ: ᐃᓄᖕᓂᒃ
ᐅᑭᐅᕆᔭᖕᒐ: 18

Inuktitut translation by Jean Kusugak

Grandparents

Seeing my grandparents
playing cards all
night, wondering if
they miss the old days
when they used to ride
horses and
chase each other.

DEWEY BRIGHT WINGS, age 16
Crow

rain inside the end of august

I.

I spent my eleventh summer
in the golden sun-stained footprints
of who my mother told me I was.
I believed her —
to the extent of what a trail of tears
our dinner table could become,
to the limits of brown faces
I saw I was related to —
my sweaty-palmed belief never grew
out of faith in the concept though,
because my skin never danced darker than I was that July,
let alone ever likened itself to the same people she tells me I
come from

II.

When you ask me who I am,
I don't know how to answer.
No response could ever sing fair
of every breath or piece of earth I was awakened from;
In the silent frozen moments of Suburbia,
I catch my grandmother's daughter
wishing she knew the new whispers of the Res
as she prepares fry bread for my brother and me.
I know what it is to be fed Indian,
to be told where I come from
on every corner of the land,
but I only understand it in English,
and even fry bread can't fill up

the spaces I know are missing inside myself,
under my roof that only comprehends
American

III.

There are pictures of me
I know my mother loves over others,
not because of beauty or truth,
but of how well history fashionably
adorns itself on my face,
or hangs evident on a jeweled neck.
And it makes me wonder how I ever looked to her before
the pictures that prove I really am her daughter,
that make her smiles more honest
because I actually look Indian,
for once

IV.

I am 16 now and have paused
amid the rubble of everyone I am —
it is summer though
that I can't help but climb
through each wilted story and photograph that has made me.
But no matter how hard I try,
the feeling of being 11, holding my mother's hand
full of blackberries,
always conquers me.
And I'm running, running
racing up past the dry heated towns

of Native Northern California,
through alcoholic family fires
that burn my tongue and torch my eyes,
I stumble across the Klamath
that will always love my brother more for his darker skin
and wilder touch;
here I am
where I am always 11,
wondering forever
what it means to be Indian,
why it is that my small voice does not seem
that it will ever be loud enough to prove I am here,
why it is that no one may ever take me seriously
when I explain the weathered trail of where I come from:
I stand hunched forever
because my father can't explain,
and no matter where I arrive,
I fear there is a part of me
who will always remain
the white river rock
haunting the brown shore and dark waves
of who my mother will always be.

LANI WILD, age 16
Karuk

Little Grandma

Dedicated in loving memory of Jeanette B. Lion Shows, 1935-2002

I watch as my little grandma slowly
walks to her room.
She grabs the remote,
she turns on the TV,
she turns to the news.

I watch as my little grandma walks
to the kitchen.
She grabs a cup of coffee
and a toast to dip.

My little grandma ain't so little,
she's taller than me.

When she answers the phone,
she tells my friends,
"It's not here."
Click. She hangs up the phone
and wobbles back to her room
to watch the news.

DESTINY STARR LION SHOWS, age 15
Crow

At Midnight

At midnight the moon is floating
in the sky, and as soon as I get up,
it seems that I am floating with the moon.

At midnight there's a whisper
in the trees, and a voice in the
woods, and these are the midnight stories.

CURTIS D. YELLOWTAIL, age 14
Crow

Answered Prayers

She was twenty years old and living on an Indian reservation. She had reached the point in her life where it came down to one grim choice, life or death. She could continue living with the pain, rage, hurt, and fear, or she could end it all and find release. She had made up her mind: she wanted release.

The girl prayed what was going to be her last prayer on the day she chose to take her life. She wanted healing and a change from reservation life. She didn't want the shame and fear from sexual abuse anymore. She wanted to fall in love, but how could she when she loathed another person's touch? Children also terrified her. She was horrified by the thought that people have no regard for a child's innocence.

There were problems outside the home as well, and it disheartened her to see the effects of them on her people. There was an off-balance seesaw on the reservation. One side had all the good, fun, and sober memories. Crime, violence, drugs, and alcohol rode on the other side. Sometimes the girl would find herself sliding back and forth on that seesaw.

Writing, drawing, painting, and making music were her true escapes. All the problems and bad memories disappeared when she immersed herself in these outlets. The girl only wanted a more stable foundation and the opportunity to better her life and home situation.

But this didn't seem possible. She walked into the woods, praying for healing, carrying the blade she intended to use. She sat under a pine tree in the middle of the woods, and terrible images of that day when she was twelve streamed through her head like a river. Her body shook from fear and from sobbing. She was about to cut her ankles, her wrists, and her throat when she heard someone approach.

"Hey, what's up?" her friend asked. She held her head down and shook her head, trying not to respond so he would leave. "I'm coming from the bar." He held out his puffy bloodstained fists. "I got into a fight."

"You want a beer?" he asked. She took the bottle that he offered. "Hey, why you shaking? What's wrong?"

She broke down crying. They shared his case of beer as she detailed some of her past. She drank the liquid but did not taste the alcohol, nor did it affect her. She did not take her life that afternoon. Instead she went home exhausted but relieved.

They talked whenever they saw each other, and she looked forward to seeing him every time. Her trust grew and she finally told him about being sexually abused by someone he knew. She was scared and almost ran away because she didn't know how he would react. She waited for him to call her a liar. When he didn't, it took her a couple of minutes to comprehend his question: "What happened?" She told him what she remembered. She sobbed tears and snot down his shirtsleeve and her knees buckled, but he held her the entire time.

When her family members had kids, it took the girl a long time to accept her nieces and nephews. But when her sister told her she was pregnant, the girl freaked out. Old memories, fear, and doubt surfaced so horribly that she feared the downward spiral again. She knew that she would never want to touch any child in the wrong way; she wouldn't be able to live with the thought of being responsible for destroying another child's innocence.

Paranoid and terrified, the girl withdrew from her family. She was restless and had constant nightmares. She woke in cold sweats as her sister's due date approached. Her mother was with her sister during labor, while the girl was at work. After a fourteen-hour labor, her niece was born. The baby weighed five pounds, fourteen ounces, almost the same as when the girl was born. Her mom came home, exhausted, and said that it was her shift, so she went to the hospital and spent the night with her sister and the baby.

Her niece was so tiny that she had to sift through the blankets to find her. She fell in love immediately. As tears coursed down the girl's face, she knew she would be all right. Whenever the baby cried, she picked her up and placed the baby's ear over her own heart. The newborn calmed down and went back to sleep. Other family members (even the new mother) had tried that method to no avail; the baby kept crying until they gave her to the girl.

The girl was introduced to a female counselor who dealt with childhood traumas. With the counselor's help, she let go of a lot of her pain, and in the process, she cried many tears. The counselor recognized her talents as a writer, artist, musician, athlete, volunteer, and scholar, so she encouraged the girl to use these as a method of healing.

That summer, she applied for college and was accepted. She imagined the new changes she would encounter: all the new faces, new places, new experiences, and new life. It was an experience she wanted and she didn't want to miss it. She knew the downside of reservation life and she didn't want to return to that. Wanting change and not wanting to live reservation life would be more than enough to sustain her.

Those few incidents solidified her belief in Usen's power. She now trusts and has faith that her prayers will be answered no matter how difficult they may be.

TANYA KEENE, age 21
Mescalero Apache, Caddo, Acoma Pueblo, Navajo

There Is No They, Only Us

They

When I feel like a
they is when they don't
talk to me.

When I feel like a they
is when they avoid me.

When I feel like a they
is when they call me
names.

When I feel like a
they is when they don't
feel sorry about what they
did.

When I feel like a they
the day feels darker.

Us

When I feel like
an us is when they
talk to me.

When I feel like
an us is when
they include me.

When there is
an us I feel happier.

When I feel like
an us the sun
shines brighter.

MONIQUE WHITE BUTTERFLY, age 13
Oglala Sioux

Drunken Demon That I Wrestle With

Four months of play time.
He beat me mentally and called me names of hatred.
Drunk . . . C'mon, drunk . . . Drink up! Drunk!
Battered, mentally bruised, scared, and unstable,
Stuck under his foot as he made me do things at his command.
I wake up sore and cannot remember last night.
Headaches, bleeding wounds and the thought of:
"What did I do last night?"
He is laughing deep within me.
I am his mask, an empty shell to get from one place to another.
Drink, and yet drink some more.
Look stoopider after every shot.
He prefers whiskey over beer.
Makes me do weird things . . . that I don't want to do.
I struggle to get free as I stagger around campus.
But I am too drunk to remember . . . He and I are
the same people.

BRANDAN T.N. MCCARTY, age 19
Makah

Not ndn enough

I want to get deep into the root of this
deep into the root of my mixed blood
my less than a quarter
too many generations back
ndn self.
They say I cannot tribally affiliate
because there is no proof
no recorded documentation
of a fullblood Choctaw woman intermarrying
with a half Irish-Jewish, half black preacher
in Louisiana
somewhere.
For me,
there are no blood quantum papers or enrollment cards
no ndn names
no feathers or intricate beadwork
jingle dresses
frybread recipes
that got passed down to me.
Besides, we look too black to be anything but
black.
People want to justify the blood
justify what it means to be half-breed
to be quarter-breed
to be part.
Not even half
but a small segment ndn
and a city ndn at that.
No tribe
No people
No name

Just a thin part of my blood splitting the skin
every time I cut myself in half
tearing heart and muscle from bone
until all I see is my reflection in red.

CARMELA THOMPSON JR., age 20
Choctaw

Traveling During Summer

Traveling during summer
and on the way, it's a trip
because my family's turning against each other
and my mom can't get a grip.
The heat's getting everyone
no one seems to wanna have fun
because it's around 80 degrees
and we're right in the path of the hot sun
the car keeps getting hot
and my mom just won't stop.
Everyone is sweating,
while I'm thinking,
"Best family vacation," not.
So anyways to me summer really sucks
and if you ever want to travel with my family,
I wish you good luck.

PHILLIP A. SNOW, age 17
Pomo

Dear Brother

Dear Brother
I miss you
I know you're far away
You don't write or call
But I think of you every day

Dear Brother
We were so close
Until you moved away
You went with Mom
Began drugs; real wrong
I wish that you had stayed

Dear Brother
You need me
You have no more competitive ways
You stopped going to school
Started to gang bang
Now the only way I can speak of you
Is hanging my head in shame
Your friends don't care, you don't either
All your Big Sis can do is look at you and stare

Dear Brother
I haven't seen you
I have no wits of where you are
Even Dad, who was disappointed, has started to show his concern
No one has seen you or heard of where you are
Mom says she tried, but she threw in the towel
You left the house in the middle of the night
Time and time again

This time you left unnoticed
Now nowhere to be found

Dear Brother
I urged you to make the right choice;
To choose to walk not trip
Choose to see not fall
It was all your choice you see, yet you made no effort at all

Dear Brother
You should stop and realize where you're headed
You're going in the wrong way
Soon your choices will be regretted
You'll wish you had listened
when you're caught in a bind
Your body gone crazy
Your mind's end of time

Dear Brother
I miss you
Although so far away
I know now where you are
Even though you're not near
Your voice I still hear

Dear Brother
You made poor choices
As you may have learned
You chose your friends over family
You had so many opportunities
With our friends you went;

Smoked pot, got shot
That didn't stop you
You need more action, but couldn't handle the satisfaction
You stole, fought, finally got caught
I want you with me, but there's a problem you see
Because your lesson in life
You have been taught

DOMINIQUE JOHNSON, age 13
Pueblo, Navajo

Ex-Con

I look at my past and I'm glad it was put to rest. Oh, yeah, I was a pest, just like some of the best. I've resisted arrest and even made a quest. If you were to look at me and said I haven't changed one bit, then you just better turn around and sit.

I'm not the same. I go around and play the game. Sometimes I may get blamed for the wrong things. The people don't care, they still see you as a con everywhere. They don't see you as you are. They just want you behind one big bar. So you sit here and pray that everything will be okay.

You get put in an 8 × 8 foot cell with someone you've never met and he's tellin' you to just get. You wonder why and you think of your girls at home and start to cry. You look at a picture of your kid. You don't get to watch him grow up because of things you did, because you got 25 to Life for pulling out a 2-foot knife. Now it's all over and I'm living at home, it's Paris in Rome. I finally got let free and everyone just let me be. So for now I'm an **Ex-con,** and Life will go on.

JOSHUA P. KLEMM, age 15
Hopi

My Favorite Runner

My favorite runner's name was Tricky, but all the street people knew him as Tricky Heights. They added Heights because that's how you say "partner" in the Kiowa language, and that's what he was to everybody. Even though he looked around forty, he was in his early thirties, but his mind was stuck in his grade-school years. He was always known to be three beers short of a six pack, but no one really knew why. Some people say he was always like that, but most say that he went on an acid trip and never came back. His dress attire could almost be proof of the acid-trip theory because it always consisted of brown slacks, a weird cowboy shirt, and shiny cowboy boots. If you ever saw the TV show *Laverne and Shirley*, he looked exactly like the character Squiggy in it, except Tricky looked all strung-out and on the verge of D.T.'s. Every time I saw him, he'd be smoking a cigarette and carrying a small radio. His hangouts were at stores, so he could bum change, and that's where I met him, the first time I asked him to buy me some beer.

"What's going on, Tricky Heights?" I asked him as I got out of my gray Cutlass, which I had just bought with my per-cap money, and tried to walk to the entrance of a ghetto convenience store called Step-N-Fetchum. I was just barely eighteen on this humid night.

"Hey, *piah-phee**, w-what are you d-doing?" asked Tricky Heights at a fast speed, which is the way he always talked.

"Nothing, just about to get the night started," I said, putting my Raiders baseball cap over my bald head, as my skinny friend, Peabody, got out of my ride.

"You g-got any change, *piah-phee?* I need to g-get some g-gas for my car. It b-broke down outside of town."

"Don't pull that shit on me, I know you ain't got a car. Just tell

* *Piah-phee is Kiowa for brother.*

me the truth and I'll hook you up, *say-gee**," I said, knowing he was lying.

"All right, *piah-phee,* I want to g-get a forty for the road, I g-got a long walk home t-to the country," said Tricky, with a smell of stale beer coming from the words he stuttered.

"You can't tell me the whole truth, can you? I know you live in Prairie Village and that's just two blocks from here."

"Sorry, *piah-phee.* You g-got some change?"

"Wait up, Thomas, maybe he can help us out on our current situation," added Peabody, who was just an average-looking eighteen-year-old Indian, except he had thick glasses, so everyone called him "Peabody," after the cartoon character Mr. Peabody.

"Hell, yeah, not a bad idea. I like the way you think. Tricky, if you go in there and buy us some beer, we'll buy you a forty, how's that?"

"Okay, *piah-phee,* b-but can you d-do something else for me?" asked Tricky, with a serious look on his unshaved face.

"What?" I asked, as I reached into my baggy jeans to pull out some money to give to Tricky.

"C-can you c-comb my hair like Elvis?"

"Comb your hair like Elvis! What kind of shit is that?" I asked and laughed in disbelief with Peabody.

"C-can you, *piah-phee?*"

"You're serious, aren't you? All right, when you get out, we'll comb your hair like Elvis," I agreed, but only 'cause we really needed the beer because we had some bitches waiting on us at a secluded spot. Tricky walked into the Step-N-Fetchum store and bought us a case of forty ounces and an extra one for himself. When he came out, barely able to carry the large box, we hid the beer in the trunk.

"So, you g-going to help m-me out, *piah-phee?*" asked Tricky, with a childlike sparkle in his eyes that I couldn't resist.

"What the hell, yeah, but let's go in the alley," I said, as Peabody and Tricky followed me.

* * *

* *Say-gee* is Kiowa for *friend.*

Tricky found a milk crate and took a seat on it, while I looked around to find something to comb his tangled hair with. Peabody was too busy laughing at Tricky and making fun of me to help find a comb, which made me a little frustrated because we were in a hurry. Finally, I found two thin branches, about a foot long apiece, and sculpted his hair with them. He just sat there as I tossed his greasy hair around like a salad. I didn't waste too much time with his grooming and finished as fast as I could.

"He looks like an Indian Elvis Presley, don't he?" I asked Peabody, who nodded his head in agreement.

"Thank you, *p-piah-phee,* th-thank you," said Tricky, as he got up and walked off with the funkiest hairdo I had ever seen.

"Let's get the fuck out of here, I can't believe I just did that."

As my adolescent days passed, my parties kept going and the demand for beer was at its highest for me. It was all good, though, because every time I needed a runner I would find Tricky at one of the stores bumming for change and he was always down to help a Native out. After a while, he even stopped charging me beer; as long as I combed his hair like Elvis, he was happy. Sometimes I would find him while I had ladies with me, and they were always curious why I had to go behind the store with him. I never did tell them why, but I knew they really wanted to know because his hair was always fucked up when we came back to the front. It was our little secret, it was our little pact.

One hot day, when I was driving around, I spotted him in an alley, next to a store. I parked my Cutlass in front of the store and walked back to ask him for his services. To my surprise, I found a good Indian friend of mine named Stephen Turtledove combing Tricky's hair like Elvis, and it offended me. Tricky started stuttering and explaining as soon as I approached them.

"They p-paying me b-back for g-getting them some b-beer, *piah-phee,*" said Tricky.

"You wanna finish?" asked Stephen, as his two-man crew laughed.

"Nah, go ahead, but can you do mine like Michael Jackson's next?" I asked, just to fuck with him.

"Fuck you, Thomas, we just trying to get us some beer. We're not trying to steal your runner."

"I hope not, 'cause this Native gets thirsty too often to not have a runner. Why don't ya'll just go and I'll finish for ya, because I need him to hook me up."

Stephen and his crew were more than happy to leave and did. After they drove off in an old, beat-up car, I asked Tricky to get me some beer. Tricky went inside the store, purchased the beer, and walked back to my car with my load. When he asked me to finish his hair, I told him I couldn't because he was fucking up and needed to chill. I explained how if he ran for other people, he would become "hot" to the cops, and they loved to bust runners like him. So, he understood after that, that it was in his best interest to be just my crew's runner.

My crew and I kept in good relations with Tricky, and after a while, everybody in my crew could comb his hair like Elvis, and I mean really like it. The word hit the streets and everybody knew he was our runner. Our relationship with him was good, to the point where we would give him money even when he didn't ask for it. We had his back, so he could go to neighborhoods he was once scared to bum in. I thought we would never have to back him up for real, until he told us that some white boys were chasing him down like an animal and shooting him with BB guns. He told us they usually got him near his neighborhood, which was Prairie Village.

One humid day, Peabody and I had nothing to do, so we drove around smoking some weed and looking for the fools, even though we didn't know who they were. We just happened to be in P.V. (Prairie Village) at the right time, and from a distance saw Tricky walking back to his mom's house. P.V. had about two blocks of nothing between it and the rest of the town, with a small road that zigzagged through it like a gray snake. He was right in the middle of that nothing and was traveling at his usual fast pace. We parked at an abandoned store that overlooked the small stretch of nothing and the brick houses that made up P.V.

Peabody and I lit another joint for our enjoyment and just sat back to watch Tricky walk, because I had a strange feeling we might get a chance to see what he was complaining about. Just as Peabody asked me what the hell we were doing, an old, dark-blue Mustang with tinted windows came blazing out of P.V., like sudden death, and sped its way toward Tricky. Before we could blink an eye, Tricky became a whole different kind of runner, a "running for his life" runner. He ran off the road, into an open plain, and toward town, like Billy Mills was running when he won the gold. The Mustang stopped where he ran off the road, and a BB-gun barrel appeared out of the driver's window. Tricky saw this and started running in zigzags all the way to the main road, which was First Street, right next to the nothing plain. Peabody and I couldn't help ourselves, so we cheered him on and then laughed because it was a funny scene. I couldn't tell if they were shooting, though, because it was a BB gun and they don't make any sound when shot.

I knew the Mustang and I knew the driver. It was a sixteen-year-old clean-cut white boy named Biff, who had white-blond hair and always wore preppy clothes. Even from a distance, I could tell he wasn't alone; he had his best friend, Lyle, who was his equivalent, with him. Biff and I had known each other for a long time, because he played football under me through my Anadarko public school years. He was a spoiled piece of shit who would probably die without his daddy, and I disliked him, which he knew, and I made him kiss my ass every time I saw him. Peabody and I reviewed the situation in our easily entertained state of mind and decided to turn the tables around to amuse ourselves even more. The Mustang sped through the nothing and caught up with Tricky in Blacktown, which was a neighborhood of rundown houses.

After pulling out of our viewpoint, we eased behind them, in a cool-like fashion, and tailed them through Blacktown, which is sometimes called "Cracktown." Tricky ran through messy yards, between crack houses, around closed buildings, and across narrow streets, as the white boys tried to get close enough to shoot him. He was giving them a run for their money, though, because he made it to the next small neighborhood, which was "the east side," and then to the fairgrounds in it. The fairgrounds had a one-way road that went in and out of it, called the Horseshoe, and that was where they finally caught him. There was no fair around, so there was only wide, open space in all directions, except for a few buildings and the grandstand, which Tricky didn't have time to make it to, which left him with nowhere to run and no way to outsmart them. Tricky stopped to surrender, and the Mustang pulled off of the one-way road and slowly onto the grass beside him. The two white boys joyfully got out of their car, walked up to Tricky, and put their arms behind his neck, like they were long-time friends. We watched from a nearby park and waited for the right time. I could tell they were congratulating him on a good chase by the way they patted him on the back, and it looked like they were giving him a choice on his punishment, as if he deserved it. It got me pissed off thinking about how many times they probably got away with fucking with Tricky and others, and how if we Indians did it to a white man, the police would show up out of nowhere to take our asses to jail for the unheard-of crime. After a brief conversation with Tricky, the two white boys blindfolded him and he marched away, as they laughed and cocked their BB guns. At that moment, we sped off toward them and surprised the hell out of them when we pulled up next to their Mustang. They recognized me, as Peabody and I got out of my car.

"Hey, what's up, Thomas?" asked Biff, whose pale skin all of a sudden turned pink, as he tried to play it cool with me because he knew something was up.

"Nada, what's up with y'all?" I asked, as I stared into their "no respect for nothing" eyes.

"We're just trying to have a little fun, check this out," said Biff in his girlish tone, and he pointed his BB gun at Tricky.

"Why you tryin' to shoot my uncle, bitch?" I yelled in a serious tone only inches from his face, as I grabbed the gun from his arms and Peabody grabbed the other one out of Lyle's arms before they could retaliate.

"Ah, dude, I didn't know he was your uncle. I'm sorry, I was just playing," apologized Biff.

"Yeah, Thomas," said Lyle, with a look on his face that made it obvious he was scared shitless. "We didn't mean no harm, they're just BB guns."

"Is that so? Uncle Tricky! Get that damn thing off and get over here!" I yelled. Tricky took the blindfold off and was real surprised to see me standing with a BB gun in my hand, rescuing him.

"Let's fuck them up, Thomas," said Peabody, who always went a little crazy off of weed.

"Now there's no need to trip, we're sorry," said Biff, as he and Lyle stood with their hands in their pockets, like they were waiting for sentencing, which they were.

"H-hey, *piah-phee*. What's g-going on?" greeted Tricky, with a smile from sideburn to sideburn.

"These the guys you said were fucking with you?" I asked, hoping he would say yes.

"Yeah, *p-piah-phee*, it's them."

"Why the fuck are y'all fucking with Indians? Y'all don't like us, or what? Fuck it, by the time we get done with y'all today, I know y'all ain't going to like us," I told the white chicken shits.

"Thomas, we don't want no shit. You can have the guns," said Biff, as they attempted to walk back to his car in a "calm down" fashion. "We're just going to go on home."

"I don't think so, Homey. The Indian don't play that shit. Y'all better get your asses back away from the car or I'm going to fuck y'all up even more," I said. They backed away quick, knowing I wasn't playing around.

"Come on, Thomas, we said we're sorry," said Lyle, with a pitiful look on his pink face that disgusted me.

"To me, but I ain't the one y'all should be apologizing to. Apologize to Tricky."

"Sorry, Tricky, we were just playing," said Biff, in a tone that gave away he really wasn't sorry, which pissed me off even more.

"I think y'all should compensate him for the damages you caused him."

"I got thirty dollars, how's that?" asked Biff.

"Yeah, *p-piah-phee,* yeah, *p-piah-phee,*" said Tricky, like it was music to his ears.

"No, something more than money."

"T-they can c-comb my hair l-like Elvis, *piah-phee,*" added Tricky, who needed his hair combed bad.

"All right, you heard him. He wants his hair combed like Elvis, so get to it, and use y'all's own combs."

"What?" asked Lyle, as if I were joking.

"You heard me, now do it."

Biff and Lyle, who both tried to hide the hatred they had for us, pulled out their fancy combs. Tricky took a seat on the hood of my car, facing my windshield. They looked over his greasy hair and started sculpting it into different parts, until finally deciding on one. After a lot of twirling, turning, and combing, they finished their creative grooming, but I wasn't satisfied with their amateur work, so I made them do it over and over. On their fourth attempt, they made a hairdo that resembled the young Elvis's, and I was impressed.

"What do you think, dog, should we let them go?" I asked Peabody.

"No, I think we should teach them a lesson," answered Peabody, who looked angrier than I was.

"All right, y'all two, turn around," I ordered.

"Why? We did what you said," snapped Lyle, like he had rights.

"Do it before I fuck y'all up," I ordered with authority.

Biff and Lyle turned their backs to us, and I handed the gun I had to Tricky, who looked like he'd waited his whole life for that moment. Peabody got in a position to fire, but I motioned him to just chill out, and he complied, knowing what was up.

"All right, Tricky, here's your chance to get these white bitches back. Go ahead and bust some BBs in their asses," I said.

"Ok-kay, *piah-phee,*" Tricky said, as he shot Biff in the ass first. After that, he went off, pumping and shooting, over and over. Peabody and I started to laugh and couldn't stop, because it was some of the funniest shit we had ever seen. Tricky unloaded the BB gun on their asses, as they tried to take the pain but flinched after every shot hit them on the ass. By the time I allowed them to turn back around, they looked like they wanted to cry.

"Do y'all see how it feels? We were just playing. We didn't mean no harm, hell, they're just BB guns," I said, as I grabbed the second full BB gun from Peabody. I pumped it up several times and, in a quick draw, shot Biff right in the balls before he could figure out what I was doing.

"Yeah, we see how it feels," said Lyle, as he protected his balls.

"Now get the fuck out of here, and if y'all want some shit over this, y'all know where to find me. Take y'alls' asses back to Regency, disrespectful pieces of shit!" I yelled, as they clumsily got back into Biff's Mustang and drove off like they wanted to get away from that memory as fast as possible. We put our new BB guns in my trunk and jumped in my ride, with Tricky. After deciding to go to the liquor store, I gave Tricky some money to get us a bottle to celebrate our small, meaningful victory. As we drove off into the horizon, I asked Tricky if he wanted us to redo his hair for his favor.

"N-no, *piah-phee,* the white b-boys d-did a real g-good job and I l-like it," he said, as his Elvislike hair flapped in the wind.

"Yeah, they did, a real good job," I said, staring at him in the backseat, with a well-showing smirk on his face.

That day, we helped our runner win a race for our race.

THOMAS M. YEAHPAU, age 21
Kiowa

I Am Native American

I am Native American
I wonder why some people don't like us
I hear voices in my head telling me that my people are wrong
I see hatred
I want us to love each other as brothers and sisters
I am Native American
I pretend we all get along
I feel hurt
I touch my skin
I worry about why other Native Americans call me white
I cry when I hear how bad my ancestors were treated
I am Native American
I say, "I love you," to my family
I dream that one day color won't matter
I try to make that dream come true
I hope that one day I will be the first woman
Native American president
I am Native American

RAMONA BILLY, age 11
Hopland Band of Pomo Indian

Old Crow Warriors

Watching the trees swaying,
the beautiful colors of leaves.
Take a breath. Can you feel
the crisp cold air enter
your lungs?

Look, look, the gray cloud.
Is there no end?
Winter is upon us.

Shhh. Hear that?
The voices, the voices
of old Crow warriors.

Hear them? They're telling
me to be strong.

FREDERICK M. HOWE III, age 17
Crow, Blackfeet

Oral Tradition

Our oral tradition isn't fading away
Just hard to recognize 'cause it has changed
Look for it hard 'cause it's hard to see
When I found it, I realized it was always with me

MOTHER
Never ever follow the little people into the woods, they'll take
    you away from me
Never date women with ticklish knees because that means
    they're boy crazy
Watch yourself in the church of Lucifer, the whole world
Find the way to the church of God, small buildings with a cross

FATHER
He was the biggest oral tradition I ever experienced
From drunken bar fights he brought home to graduations he
    never attended
Success and change scared him, I won't be his successor
He showed me how not to live, I'll never play softball, ever

GRANDMA
"Jesus is coming back someday, even though the white society
    still won't allow him in public, so look for him on a rez,
    aaayyyeee!"

GRANDPA
"Kone! When things get down, this song is all you need:
        Daw-khaih-yee, my -lord, daw-khaih-yee
        Daw-khaih-yee, my -lord, daw-khaih-yee . . ."

Uncles

Apaches — don't bring up Geronimo
Comanches — can't take a joke
Sioux — think Black Hills is land they owned
Cheyenne — not down with dog jokes
Quarter Cherokees — Well, you know
Choctaws — love a good joke

Aunts

Kiowa girls — only trust 'em as much as you trust yourself,
   they read their men like books
Comanche girls — can't be trusted
Apache girls — they're all right
Navaho girls — will nurture you the best
Sioux girls — are always up to something
Cheyenne girls — like to stand by their man,
   but only if the man is always there

Friends

Chief Passes Out always tells the tale of when he passed out on
   a floor furnace, then walked around for a week with a
   checkered face, *remember*
Chief Drinks-a-Lot always tells the tale of when he had sex
   with a shapeshifter at a 49, then she turned into a beer and
   they have been in love ever since, *whatever*
Chief Blowing Smoke always tells the tale of the night he was
   staggering home and a cop picked him up and took him home
   for his safety, *no one believes him*

MYSELF

From a new generation of storytellers, a whole different breed
Telling of women I had to conquer and men I
   didn't have to defeat
My story: a boy from the land of no self-esteem to
   a man with a college degree
Telling my kids, "It takes a lot of hard work and sacrifice to
   be what you want to be."

THOMAS M. YEAHPAU, age 22
Kiowa

You Stole My Words
Heartbreaks

You stole my words
  The only value I carried in my hands
Took them
  Using them as currency to buy whatever you pleased.

I would have given them to you
  For free. If you had only asked. Instead,
Scraped from the pores of my skin
  Torn from the pink of my tongue.
You took them.

I can't imagine what my words could do for you
  Except fill up space in your dusty corners
Or give you sentences that float in your mind when you walk
  alone. But they gave me everything.

Then again, it is my fault.
  I showed you how they shined and felt,
Weighing down the pockets of my dress.
  It is my fault I showed you their beauty.

Why did you take them?
  I would have given them to you for free.
We would have both been better off.
  I would still have my best friend and you would still have me.

Vena A-dae, age 19
Kiowa, Cochiti

Disease

Oh, how angry you make me
with your careless, selfish authority
like a disease you spread your hatred
what beautiful lands and waters
  you've wasted
you think you can "buy" it
want to "own" it
emptiness fills your soul
you try to take it
  tear it down
it's time you pay the "toll"

T. Marie Hart, age 17
Red Lake Band of Ojibwe

65-Adam

All my life livin' on the rez tryin' to understand what the
government says.
All I ever hear is lies, it makes me want to sit down and cry.
They always be puttin' us in a position where we can't do
anything but live off their provisions.
Frustration sets in our minds, we give up hope and let anger
make us blind.
We try to forget, get lost in our little bit.
We stop the thought that should be taught to the masses,
so when the day comes we can all get our passes.
Passes, what?!? you say, it won't matter because it will all
be in dismay.
No one will know what truth to obey.
But this is what they want us to think, keeping us away from
knowing we are a true link.
A link to the past and future, we must show them we are
more than a movie feature.
Like I've said before, we must wage an intellectual war.
Prove that we are the true scientific thinkers, not low-down
dirty drinkers.
For many of us that's just a cover-up, because of the many ways
we've tried, it only made us give up.
My words may sound contradicting, but can you see, I'm doing
my best with all my thinking.
We must really think before we act, so when it ends, we won't
seem like rats.

We need to quit giving up and throw away our secret cover-ups. After we have thought things through, we must show them what we as a unified nation can do.

NATHANIEL BORDEAUX, age 19
Sicangu, Oglala Lakota

Why the Indians Never Won

In the movies the Indians never win.
Even though you never see John Wayne smile,
It's always the pale faces winning.
We always get shot or there's too many of them.
The Indians never win.
When Geronimo fought, he never won.
When Sitting Bull fought, he never had a chance.
So why is it the Indians never win?
We are a red clan and they don't like it
They are so blinded by the greed and hatred,
They don't see any pity in their dark hearts at all.
The Indians never win.
We are the only ones who never win.
You can watch the same movie over and over.
You can pray and pray for us to win but we don't.
The Indians never win.

MARY REDHOUSE, age 16
Pyramid Lake Paiute, Walker River Paiute, Wind Rock Navajo

We Finally Won

When Custer came we were ready
Ready to fight.
Ready to protect our family
Ready to rewrite history
Sitting Bull, Geronimo, Tonto
were ready to fight
Custer came
He came in our dreams
He came in our visions
When he came, he rode
He rode over our mountains
He rode through our trees
He rode over our mother
He came over the mountains
Like a white cloud, his soldiers
Wearing armor
Our warriors only wearing
Red, yellow, and black, colors flashing
Brightly and proud
The beautiful scars from hunting
They were beautiful and strong
Their hair black and long and braided
They stood there looking stoic
Proud, and Indian.
Custer charged with all his might
We captured him and made him watch
As we killed his soldiers slowly then
We killed him slowly and painfully
Wearing his white body as a trophy
Scalped. We hung his heart in the trees

For the vultures to eat.
We had won.

Mary Redhouse, age 16
Pyramid Lake Paiute, Walker River Paiute, Wind Rock Navajo

For the Children

Dedicated to the men who fought Cochiti Lake

Cochiti cried
to me
    40 years before I was born

He cried
    Spilling his history across lost acres
    Beneath water
        That clogged the life of his only people
    The children
    The children

Cochiti prayed
with me
    While old men in Levis rolled two inches
    Above the ankles
    Muddy socks
        Grew strength from their hands and heart
        Blossomed from their mouths
            Like watermelon in the lonely fields
    For the children
    For the children

For me
Cochiti saved
    The memories
        Offered like candy
    Of paradise
        Born from the bodies of
        The old ones
        Who try to reconstruct

The right ways
Through their stories
Only to protect us
Hoping someday
We will all be children again

VENA A-DAE, age 20
Kiowa, Cochiti

In the Nicotine Kitchen

When I look
into my pawpaw's eyes

I see him sitting
in a nicotine kitchen

smoking & drinking
from a difficult life.

When his hands
touch the beer can

I can feel the world
ending, his gray hair

a smoke of cloud
wandering off.

JENNIFER MORNINGSTAR, age 15
Navajo

That Night

I can still feel my feet being so cold I can still smell the smoke in the air I can still see myself crying for my mother's help I can still see myself sitting by the heater trying to get warm and trying to get away from them I can still remember trying to hide all my fears I can still feel the hands on my body I can still feel myself fighting them off of me I can still feel myself shaking and rocking I can still feel myself being scared to even close my eyes to sleep I can remember the weather it was a cold night it was rainy and foggy the sky was so dark the moon was so bright and it was half I remember the night feeling like it was never going to end I can feel myself slipping away from my body and from my own self I can still feel myself feeling like I was dirty I remember the feelings that I had the next day the pain the blame the being treated and the loss of a friendship that I thought I could count on I remember the thought of telling my mom and dad what were they going to think about me there are no words that can tell how I felt at the time and no words that could explain it I could remember it like it was yesterday.

Within Yourself

There was a soul that could not eat sleep talk think or even walk at times I was this soul at one time in my life I was depressed I would sometimes lay in bed at night turning and twisting but could not sleep I would wake up in a sweat even if it was daytime I would not want to eat but had to make myself eat and when I did eat I would get sick I was full of anger and didn't know what to do with it so I took it out on everyone and when they got mad at me I would start to hate them but it was not them it was me I would not like to be around people and when I was really not there I was off in my own little world as long as I was not in reality but the hardest part is to speak up and ask for help but believe me when you do it will be healing for yourself and for others.

Deep Inside

My heart was broken and my days were gone and I lost the feeling of my heart I had given my heart to so many people that I loved and they gave me nothing back but a heart that became like a stone so I find it hard to trust anyone but myself because I don't want to get hurt anymore and when someone tells me to open up all they are going to get is a stone that will break and turn into nothing but anger and hate but don't be mad because there will be a day when I can love once more like I used to it's just that I need time to get out the hate and anger that I have and it won't take a week or a month but it's going to take a while so don't hate me for what I have to deal with.

DESIREE GARCIA, age 16-17
Pomo

This Is Part of Me I Hate

I am a man of hatred and anger and only toward myself.
Why am I a man of such words?
Simply because I hate myself for the mistakes of my past.
They dig into my shoulders like the teeth
  of a gray wolf of the wild.
The anger chews on my head like a black bear.
I try to fight them off with my bare hands
But my hands are soft as waterlogged clay.
Can it be that they have beaten me?
Nah . . . Just because I am down . . . don't count me out just yet.
::wicked laugh as he is being mauled
  by his bear and wolf demons::

BRANDAN T.N. McCARTY, age 19
Makah

Home

The air was still, as if to say in its own words, *You know the answer,* like a whisper. A slight breeze shook the leaves. I sat on the porch of a place I called home. A place that was called home because it was the only place that made me safe yet so insane. A place where my family slumbered, cried, fought, yelled, screamed, laughed, and loved. Returning seemed like the hardest thing that I had ever done. I never knew I would return to this place. I guess I really never knew as many of the answers of living as I thought I knew. Home was a place where you could walk out any door, look out of any window and see the beauty of nature. It was a place I took for granted, never really appreciating it until I was gone.

NICOLETTE E. KURIP, age 20
Ute

foundry

the fat hook plummeted from 30 feet above
scarring your eye purple
stunning the air from your lungs

how many times
have burning shame-tears steamed
your eyes behind plates of plastic
rendering them to unfeeling steel?

how many times
(after the sparks licked up and gnawed in)
have you stood naked
counting patches of milky pearlized skin
seared into the tanned leather of your limbs?

how many times has the cruel uniform been replaced?
have you started to count the helmet
as part of your skeleton?

my brother
who runs stronger than the yellow medicine river
have you buried your dreams so far behind
you've forgotten
your promise to excavate them someday?
you said you would dig them up
hold them in the curve of your palm
small and precious as your first son's tears

brave brother
when you look out with still tender eyes
try to remember those tears
he cried them for you

please don't be too brave
strong running brother

SHANNAH ANDERSON, age 21
Anishinaabe

Holding On to the Past

Giving thanks for all creation, I place my pinch of tobacco at the base of the old pine tree, and continue on the Red Road to another day of classes.

I go to school in western Massachusetts, over a thousand miles away from the Leech Lake Reservation, my home. My name is Clarence "Duane" Meat; I am Arapaho/Ojibwe Indian and the only indigenous person in the private school I attend.

Before prep school, I went to the Bug-O-Nay-Ge-Shig school in Bena, Minnesota, from kindergarten to eighth grade, where the administration stressed the importance of Native American tradition. Now surrounded by elitism and wealth, I realize the wisdom and intelligence of my elders' teachings. Not until that radical change in environment did tradition make complete sense.

I strive to walk the Red Road every day, trying not to be too bad or too good. It is harmful for someone to burden the spirit with malevolence or conceit. Every day, before I go to breakfast, I walk outside into the cool morning air and pray to the Creator. My elders say that we must respect life because everything in this world contains a life force. They say to put out tobacco every morning in appreciation for each new day, for those things that gave their spirits to the next world for our survival, and for the gifts that the Great Spirit has given each of us.

When I grasp the shreds of tobacco in my hand, the scent evokes images of my ancestors sitting upon the ground in a circle, laughing and talking.

When I am so far away from home, I like to remember the elders conversing in Ojibwe, discussing our values, telling stories, or giving encouragement. Usually, they must translate into English for me, but just the sound of my language fills me with pride. My elders say words are sacred. Every word we speak reaches the ears of the Great Mystery and our ancestors. They watch over us, helping us through the tough times if we are willing to listen.

My tribal names, Misaabi and Hay she nah chay, connect me with my spirituality and my forebears. In addition, each one of our original languages is the most valuable asset we have in resisting assimilation. However, the languages will only exist as long as we speak and sing them.

Being far from home, I miss certain things I took for granted as a young boy. The excitement of the powwow revitalizes my spirit after migrating through the society of our prolonged visitor. The drums, the bells, the visiting remind me of the tribal cohesion, the happiness of our people as we celebrate our traditions. When the jingle of the bells synchronizes with the beat of the drum, I can feel my heart beating simultaneously with Mother Nature's.

Sitting down and doing homework, I sometimes let my mind wander. During my contemplation, I ponder and hypothesize about the future of the reservation. What can I do as an individual? I plan to follow the teachings of my people.

Life is a circle. My traditional teachers say that life flows in a cycle, from infant to adult to elder to infant. The sun, the moon, the earth, the stars, the drum, the hoop, the medicine wheel, and the powwow ring also form circles. The elders say to respect these things or the Great Spirit will not give us anything else, or possibly take away what has already been given.

Thinking of the old lessons, I remember the ceremonies the elders diligently perform every year for us young knuckleheads. I hope one day to be able to fill those moccasins. I recall the sweat lodge in particular, and especially the incredible heat that envelopes your face and scorches your throat when the water hits those ancient spirits the rocks. The feeling is empowering, yet many of my peers pass by the powerful gift of culture.

We are losing our tradition. In some parts, the reservation looks like a forgotten borough of the inner-city ghetto. Besieged by modern excessiveness, the "Rez" becomes increasingly hopeless. Alcohol not only affects the user, but also destroys communities and families. I always hear that our culture can save us, but to some, the culture has become nothing more than a marketing tool or a symbol of a bygone existence. Slogans will not reverse the damage of one hundred years. Therefore, the children must learn in detail the greatness of their heritage.

Spirituality has ensured the survival of American Indian people since the genesis. The Great Mystery placed our ancestors upon this plentiful continent and gave them the strength to survive a holocaust. Our ancestors remembered the importance of nature by keeping in balance with their environments. The early visitors marveled at our culture and the "noble" society that our ancestors established, eventually using it as the basis of modern democracy. The influence of Turtle Island resounds through the debates of Congress, the voices of feminists, and the clamor of environmental picket lines. Nevertheless, modern society has only fabricated our cultures, not adopted them, and thus they deteriorate with each passing second. The old ways are safety lines — waiting for us to grasp them.

Protection of the old ways was worth the lives of many before us, lost in countless battles and massacres. I will continue the heritage and teach my children to cherish their culture.

CLARENCE D. MEAT, JR., age 17
Cheyenne and Arapaho Tribes of Oklahoma

I Wonder

I learn a lot just by
listening to my grandfather's stories
and watching his eyes light up every time
he sees his grandchildren.
But I have always wondered why ol' gramps
always wakes up extra-early and looks out
the picture window just to watch the sunrise
while he sips on his straight black coffee.
He's always crazy like that.
I wonder how grandfather will feel, blowing out
sixty candles on his sixtieth birthday next Sunday.
I wish I lived in my grandfather's day,
when soda pop was only a nickel
and everyone ate pickles!

HILLARY REED, age 15
Crow

Big Foot

One Friday afternoon, I asked my Grandpa to give me a ride to the foot of the mountains so I could go hunting. He agreed, loaned me his gun, and dropped me off at the foothills of the Little Rockies. By the time I arrived, it was already 4:00 P.M., and I realized that I only had three shells. As I got ready to jump out of Grandpa's truck, he asked me, "What time do you want me to pick you up?"

"It's okay, Gramps, I'll just walk home."

I remember how lonely I felt as I watched him drive away, but I then thought of the freedom I had in the mountains. Oh, man, I really felt good! I turned to walk up the mountains, thinking of my three shells and the hour and a half of sunlight I had left. There was a whitetail doe not far from where I was walking, and I stopped to measure out the distance. Then I fired a shot and I felt really good because I got a kill. I ran over to make sure she was dead. She was, so I covered her with brush and started to walk home.

There was four coulees that I had to cross over to get home. I had this awful feeling that something was following me. The feeling grew more and more intense the farther I walked. It was like eyes were watching me, and I could smell this foul odor. The first thing I thought was that a mountain lion was stalking me. After about three-fourths of a mile, I stopped dead in my tracks. I had a really expensive night scope on the gun that my grandpa let me use. I lifted up the gun, placed the stock into the crevice of my shoulder, and prepared the gun for firing. I turned slowly, expecting to see a mountain lion, but it was something else. As I gazed at this thing, I began to raise the scope and seen a lot of black hair, and then I seen the upper torso of this scary but beautiful creature. It had a very stern gaze. At a distance of about fifty yards or so to the south of my location, there was a Big Foot,

Sasquatch, whatever you want to call him/her. He was standing the same way a person stands when they are startled, or like a defensive football player. I immediately dropped the gun and started to run north, in the direction of my house. Then I heard a wrenching holler, like a growl and a loud cry mixed together. I didn't stop to look at him a second time. I just ran faster than I had ever run before.

That night, I slept on the floor of my Grandpa's cabin, and awoke in the morning to Grandpa asking for his gun. I told him the story, but I seen a ray of disbelief in Grandpa's face. Later, I took him to the place that I dropped the gun. The gun was there, but it was all broke up, like something that had been put through a grinder. The barrel was bent at about a ninety-degree angle, and the scope, stock, and grips were destroyed. I looked at the gun and glanced at Grandpa, and he said, "Let's get the hell out of here."

On the way home, Grandpa said, "Don't worry about the gun or scope, they can be replaced, but you, well, we kinda need you around."

I knew what he meant by that, but it didn't ease the tension I felt. I don't know if Big Foot would have hurt me, but I'm glad that he chose the gun.

— This is a true story, told by a true Native with true feelings about a true subject that is not fake.

VINCENT F. WHITE, age 20
Assiniboine, Little Shell Chippewa, Banic, Cree, Gros-Ventre

Eeling

A willow pole long and straight
Barbless hooks peeled and shaped.

A warm breeze says the time is right
Uncle and I will eel tonight.

The sun is setting, night draws near
The time for eeling is almost here.

I hear the river far below
The trail is long, steep, and slow.

A small fire glows to cook our catch
The first eel caught is always best.

Two for me and two for him
The rest go to Elder men.

JOHNNY W. ERICKSON, age 14
Yurok

My Love

Jan, Jan, how do I love thee?
Who said I did?
As I ask you to be my fry bread queen,
you give a snarl, deep and mean.
I hear your sweet voice,
even though it gives me goose bumps.
I see the yellow sun in your teeth.
When you smile I see your razor-sharp teeth
trying to bite me, but I still love
my fry bread queen, even though she's kind of mean.
I ask you to the prom, then you
tell your mom to kill me.
I get away, but I still love thee,
my fry bread queen.

BYRON "DIRK" LITTLE LIGHT, age 16
Crow

In memoriam

Indian Ballers

Indian ballers are the best
Because of their teamwork and offense.
They rock the courts on the rez

Proving to others in the West
That their skills are built on confidence.
Indian ballers are the best.

They play for more, not for less,
Rebounding, shooting, playing defense.
They rock the courts on the rez.

Indian ballers are the leaders of the West,
Hearing the coach lecturing about offense.
Indian ballers are the best.

Beating teams like a simple test,
Together, a team, in the 3B conference,
They rock the courts on the rez.

A dream, a legend, what's the rest?
Scaring away all the upcoming opponents.
Indian ballers are the best.
They rock the courts on the rez.

LARRIS DAYNE MALE BEAR, age 17
Crow

Tough Style Rez

Everything on the Rez is kinda cool.
Things would be better if we had a pool.
When we're at school, I guess it's okay.
We all should know it's not a time of play.
Our reservation doesn't get much attention.
Why do things have to be this way?
Most Native crafts are made of clay.
All this racism makes Indians cry.
And people besides Natives wonder why.
We eat fry bread with beans.
Once in a while, we may even add cheese.
Now I'm about to end this poem.
I'm going back to the Rez,
The toughest most rugged place you'll ever be.
Imagine yourself if you were me.

SHARLA FLOREZ, age 18
Pyramid Lake Paiute

Next Generations

Through the cold
winter nights,
as these days go by,
we all sit by the fire
wondering if there's
a future ahead of us
where the young ones
will speak the
Crow language, and
where they will go
through life with
their Crow culture.

When the night is
gone and the day is
still coming,
we will be taken away
from this earth.
We will be rising as
the next generation
is coming.

When our generation is
gone, the next generation
will come, they will
come with a good
education and
we will communicate
with them through
the earth.

MARCIA BLACKSMITH, age 13
Crow, Lakota

Woman

There is a woman coming down the snowy road in
   moccasins.
Cold and as pale as the sky on a cloudy day, she shivers.
Holding a basket in one hand, she huddles to herself to
   keep warm.
She becomes colder and colder, then falls.
As her knees hit the hard, frozen ground, she looks up
   and says,
"It will not always be like this.
Times will get better.
It will not always be like this."

She has hope. Hope for the future of her people.

SARAH JERABEK, age 18
Lumbee

When

Close your eyes,
go back to the day
when the buffalo still roamed,
when the deer were plenty
in our own back yard.
Children playing, women cleaning,
men out hunting, elders laughing.
The smell of venison in the air.

Then there is silence and everything is gone.
The faint cries and shouts
are all that are left.
All you see is the way it is,
not the way it was or should
have been.

DESTINY STARR LION SHOWS, age 16
Crow

When We Are Gone

When all the lonely places
no longer exist
When the last of creation
falls
to a busy corner
I'll taste the memory of you
in the running of fresh water
I'll feel you call me there
and I'll whisper to you
still
"I remember"
the leaf said to the redwood

Angela, age 22
Cherokee, Iroquois

My Friend

When my friend died, everybody cried. The thing was, I started to do more with his father; some people didn't even bother. About two days after his death I seen an eagle flying over his father's house. I started to talk to him and he told me that his son came back one night and woke him up asking for a glass of orange juice. He gave it to him and he drank it, then left. Every day now there is an eagle that follows him everywhere he goes. It's a bald eagle to give guidance for which direction to take. It's for all of our sakes.

Joshua P. Klemm, age 15
Hopi

What Dreams May Come

People's dream for me
is for me to become a successful RCMP officer.
If this dream would come true,
then I would be one of the very first women in Nunavut
to be a female RCMP officer.

My father's dream for me
is just to follow my own dreams.
He wants me to enjoy life as much as possible
and to travel the world.

But I do have my own dreams.
I want to become a midwife here in Nunavut.
That is my dream.
I would be so proud to be able to deliver
a new and beautiful child into this world.

Dreams come in many different sizes.
It's totally up to you to make that dream come true.

JODY ROACH, age 18
Inuk

What Dreams May Come

ᐊᒃᓱᕇᑎᒥᔭᖅᐳᑦ ᑕᐅᑐᑦᕇᖅᑕᖅᐳᑦ

ᐃᓄᖕᓄᑦ ᐊᒃᓱᕇᑕᐅᔪᑦ ᐅᕙᒻᓄᑦ ᑐᕇᖕᒐᔪᑦ
ᐃᓄᖕᓄᑦ ᐳᑭᖅᑕᓕᖕᒍᕐᑯᔭᐅᓪᓗᖕᒐ ᐊᒃᓱᕇᑕᐅᔪᖕᒐ ᐳᑭᖅᑕᓕᑦᑎᐊᕙᐅᔪᓐᓇᕐᑯᑉᓗᖕᒐ.
ᐳᑭᖅᑕᓕᖕᒍᕋᔭᕐᓂᕆᒪ,
ᓯᕗᓪᓕᖅᐸᐅᕐᑲᑕᐅᕐᑲᑕᐅᓇᔭᖅᑐᖕᒐ ᐊᕐᓇᓂᒃ
ᓄᓇᕗᒥ ᐳᑭᖅᑕᓕᖕᒍᓯᒪᔪᓂᕐ.

ᐊᑖᑕᒪ ᐊᒃᓱᕇᑎᖕᒐ ᐅᕙᒻᓄᑦ ᑐᕇᖕᒐᔪᖅ
ᐊᒃᓱᕇᑎᑐᒥᔭᒻᓂᒃ ᐱᔪᒪᔭᒻᓂᒃ ᐱᓇᓱᐊᕐᑯᑉᓗᓂᖕᒐ,
ᕐᑯᕕᐊᓱᕐᑯᔮᖕᒐ ᐱᔪᓐᓇᕐᓂᓗᒃᑖᒻᓂᒃ ᐊᑐᕐᓗᖕᒐ
ᐊᒻᒪᓗ ᓄᓇᕐᔪᐊᕐᒥ ᓇᒍᓗᒃᑖᖅ ᐃᖕᒥᕐᕋᔭᕐᑯᑉᓗᓂᖕᒐ.

ᑭᓯᐊᓂᓕ ᓇᖕᒥᓂᖅ ᐊᒃᓱᕇᑎᒥᔭᒻᓂᒃ ᐅᕙᒻᓄᑦ ᑐᕇᖕᒐᔪᒥᒃ ᐱᑕᕐᑲᖅᑐᖕᒐ.
ᐃᕐᓂᓱᒃᓲᕈᖕᒍᕆᒪᔪᒐ ᑕᒡᕙᓂ ᓄᓇᕗᒥ.
ᑕᒡᕙ ᐊᒃᓱᕇᑎᒥᔭᕋ ᓱᕗᓂᒃᓴᒻᓂ.
ᓴᓇᒪᓱᑦᑎᐊᕋᔭᕋᒪ ᐃᕐᓂᓱᒃᑎᑦᑎᒍᒪ
ᓄᑕᕋᓖᑯᓗᖕᒥᒃ ᐱᐅᑦᑎᐊᕐᒥᒃ ᐱᐅᑦᑎᐊᖅᑐᒥᒃ ᓴᖅᑭᑎᑦᑎᓗᖕᒐ ᓄᓇᕐᔪᐊᕐᒧᑦ.

ᐊᒃᓱᕇᑎᒥᔭᖅᐳᑦ ᑕᐅᑐᕐᕇᖅᑕᖅᐳᑦ ᕐᑲᓄᐃᑦᑐᑐᐃᓐᓇᑦᑎᐊᖕᒍᔪᓐᓇᖅᑐᑦ.
ᐃᒻᕕᑦ ᑭᓯᒥ ᐊᒃᓱᕇᑎᒥᔭᑎᑦ ᑕᐅᑐᕐᕇᖅᑕᑎᑦ ᓴᖅᑭᑎᑦᑐᓐᓇᖅᑕᑎᑦ.

ᔩᑎ ᕇᑦᔭ
ᐅᑯᓇᖕᒫᖅᑐᖅ· ᐃᓄᖕᓂᒃ
ᐅᑭᐅᓇᔭᖕᒐ: 18

Inuktitut translation by Jean Kusugak

Living in Two Worlds

Being Native American is kind of tough, trying to live the good way as taught by our Elders and parents. At times, you want to do something because your friends are doing it, even though you know it's not right, just wanting to fit in.

Being Native American with our own culture and tradition, we are supposed to live a life that teaches respect, generosity, and bravery.

For many it's hard to live that type of life these days, with all the violence, alcohol, drug abuse, and child and spouse abuse, which are not part of our culture. We are taught children and elders are sacred and that we are to respect each other.

It makes me really scared at times, but I know that I will be safe just living the best way I can.

JESSIE LITTLE FINGER, age 11
Sioux

❄ ❄ ❄

i've been flying my whole life,
from destination to destination,
just trying to survive.
                    i worry about nothing.
i've always been taken care of by the Earth.
I'm flying with no particular destination in mind.
i'll just see where my wings take me.

SUNNY RASMUSSEN, age 18
Lac du Flambeau, Bad River Ojibwe

Window of Dreams

I look through my window into a field of dreams. This is a place where dreams can come true. It is a way to the future — not just any future but yours, mine — anybody's future.

This field holds the nutrients that make things grow and strive to reach the sky. Soil is life, from which all things come. Without it, everything dies. This is what we call Mother Earth.

Blue is the sky, which is unlimited to any bounds. The stars are never ending. They go on into infinity. The sky is unyielding, open to everyone and every animal on earth.

My window is an open door to nature that is free to grow wild, to be and do anything. Nature that is fresh and pure, where nothing can harm. Nature that is beautiful and holds all the trees, flowers, animals, and other critters who abound in this world.

This is my window of dreams. If I will dream of success, I can do anything.

TELLIE PARKER, age 22
Occaneechi Band of the Saponi Nation

Giving All I Got

It was in the fall of 1991 that I saw the guitar of my dreams. I saw it in a catalog my mom used to order clothes from. I didn't know the name brand of the guitar, but I had this particular shape running through my head. The best way I can describe it is, it looked like a crab. It was the same color as a crab, too. It wasn't a real guitar, it was a cutout, but back then, I still had an imagination. After my mom and I had a long talk about the fake, red cardboard cutout guitar, we ordered it. Day in and day out, I'd stand in front of the mirror and imitate Chuck Berry and Ritchie Valens. I had the movements down to a fine art. I'd shake it, strum, and play with my teeth.

When I was in the seventh grade, I remember waiting for the UPS man to deliver my new guitar — a real guitar. The guitar was jet black. I asked my mom for a white one, but she told me, "I won't buy you a white guitar, you might get it dirty." The dream of becoming famous like Ritchie Valens ran through my mind constantly. That summer of '91, my cousin and I watched *La Bamba* every day. It was a movie that we never seemed to get bored with. One day we watched it twice in a row. The feeling I remember most is being happy. I knew that if I poured my heart out on my guitar, I'd be good. I was pretty sure that I'd be famous like Ritchie.

When age seventeen passed, I started thinking: I am as good as Ritchie is. The only difference is, he got a break and I didn't. It sounds like I was saying, "Oh, poor me." I don't ever want to sound like that. The only difference between him and me was he made his break. I thought I could do that, too. The question was how.

I have this friend who is the best singer in the world. He can hear a song on the radio once and be able to re-create it Jam-style.

His name is Jam, short for James. He happens to be a youth minister back home on the reservation. I remember the first time I met this rock-and-roll priest. My cousin Eugene and myself were shooting pool at the local arcade. That was always fun. Playing pool is the one thing I remember very well. I would go into the arcade daily and shoot pool. I shot so much, the manager would hand me the keys so I could play and not pay a dime.

Well, one day while we were shooting pool, this skinny white guy came strutting into the arcade. He asked, "Do you do poetry, or know of anyone who does music or anything?" Feeling like a shy Native, I felt a sudden hesitancy come over my body. I didn't utter a word about playing guitar. My mom, music teacher, and friends tell me I am an excellent player, but for some reason I don't believe them.

"Shane plays excellent guitar," Eugene mentioned loud as ever.

"Man, I don't want anyone to know about that, okay?" I said. It was too late. Jam had already invited both of us to his monthly open-mic youth talent show. I was nineteen at the time. I felt old. I wasn't a youth. I didn't consider myself a youth. I guess Jam had been putting on the open-mic shows for some time. He held them at the Catholic church. I thought, "I don't know about them Catholic peoples, especially a strange white guy. Well, perhaps I might stop by that church and give this guy a chance." There I was making excuses again.

Jam went on about the "Hard Coffee Rock Youth House." Now that sure was a long name. "Have you ever sat in a coffeehouse?" Jam asked. "Well, that is exactly how I set it up," he said. We started talking about guitars and I told him that I was interested in singing. Only problem was I've never sung before. Also I was shy about playing guitar. I used to play in high school band. During the concerts I would sit way in the back and hide from the crowd. Ugh, the thought of that makes me queasy, even now. But, I decided to migrate on over to the Catholic church.

The day was warm, the sun was shining brightly, the grass was green, it was an all-around beautiful day. I had a déjà vu kind of feeling. It felt like I'd been there, done that, perhaps even dreamed it. I purposely forgot my guitar. As I walk in the church, I saw a round mirror ball on the ceiling. My eyes slowly got used to the soft light of the candles, and Jam was sitting on a wooden barstool. He was reciting a poem that he wrote called "Rez Life." The poem hit the life right-on. The people there were nice. Sitting in the front row was my friend Melissa, who is very beautiful. Her hair is long and coal-black, her skin is light, and she has hazel eyes.

I felt overwhelmed by her presence. She smiled at me and said, "Hi, Shane, how are you today?" I somehow swallowed, found my voice, and said, "Huhlo." All of a sudden I felt warm, not hot, but warm.

As soon as he was finished reading, Jam ran over to shake my hand. "Hi, I am glad you could make it. Did you bring your guitar?" he asked.

"Forgot it," I said.

"We are just starting," he said. "I read the opening poem, and I am gonna sing a song. There are snacks at the table over there."

My original plan was to go in, check it out, see if anyone was there, and then quietly leave. I didn't even notice the nice little snack table.

"I really should get gone now, Mr. Jam," I said. By this time, my legs were freezing from the air-conditioned, dimly lit church.

On hot days I liked to wear my nice cranberry-colored basketball trunks. It sucked when I hung out in cold places. I left thinking, and kind of hoping, "Next time will be cool, I will not forget my guitar." I wanted to show off in front of Melissa. I wanted her to see me play guitar, I wanted her to ask me out for dinner. After that experience, the month of June seemed to creep by ever so slowly. One good thing I'd been doing, though, was learning some current hits. I'd only been playing Metallica; it was the only thing I could play. I was pushing myself and it was a change, a good one.

Only problem was I should have taken that opportunity with

Melissa when I had the chance. Since that day I saw her, she had left for the Army. I was bummed out. If it had been possible, I'd have given myself a good ass-whooping. Thinking about it, she lived on the same block as me. I could have found my way to her front step, by accident, of course. I could picture it — I throw a ball at her window, hoping it was her window and not her mom's or anyone else's room. Melissa peeks out the window, thinking it's her bro throwing a ball at her window to get on her nerves. That's when she sees me standing outside her window, holding a box of chocolates.

"Hi," she says. "How's it going?"

I say, "I was in your neighborhood, and I thought I'd stop by to say hi."

But there was no use thinking about that. Jam was hosting another open-mic night, and I didn't want to miss that window. All month long I'd been practicing singing. Only thing was I was still self-conscious, and all of a sudden, instead of just being shy to play my beloved axe, I was shy to sing. As I got ready for the open mic, I was thinking, "Why am I scared?" I pushed my inhibitions aside. I eventually broke it down to a choice. That's what being scared is — it's a choice. With this thought in mind, I moseyed on down to the Catholic church.

Jam had it set up the exact same way as last time. But that day I was prepared for everything. I didn't forget my guitar, and I was even wearing my blue jeans. The only missing element was, of course, Melissa. As I hooked up all the cables, I wondered who was going to be at the Youth Show. The house opened at six o'clock, and it was empty.

I asked Jam, "Who all is going to show?"

He responded, "The people of God."

Every month, he hangs up the open-mic posters. He hangs up the posters every month like everyone is gonna show. At that open mic, nobody had showed so far. That only made it easier for me. The first song I performed was an oldie. I knew it well, because

I'd rehearsed it for a month. I had really been hoping that Melissa could hear it. I sang, "Oh, pretty woman." And I sang it and sang it. I couldn't get it right. That's when Jam gave me a hint.

"Just give it all you got, shout it out, who cares? It's fun."

By then, I'd realized that if I didn't give it all I got, I was going to lose out on a lot of stuff.

SHANE BRUGUIER, age 22
Cheyenne River Sioux

Solitary

Twisting and turning, yet it remains silent.
Barely breaking the ocean's surface, it is touched by light.
A mere piece of driftwood has traveled the sea waters,
seen all the sights, withheld many secrets.

How many stories lie beneath those dark ridges?
Tomorrow, a mother will die.
Next week, a new baby will be born.
This small obsolete piece of wood contains endless
  memories.

It will encounter many creatures with more stories
  to share.
Carvings cover its body from a time beyond our knowing,
to a time beyond our reach.
Solitary but never alone . . .

TARA J. REEL, age 19
Arapaho

Acknowledgments

The outpouring of submissions for this book was due to a grass-roots effort throughout the country to collect writings by American Indian youth and to notify potential contributors. Countless people were involved, from coast to coast, and from the Deep South to the Arctic. We apologize if some names have been inadvertently left off.

Our consultant, Patrick Lewis, a history major at Stanford University, helped us at every stage. His insights into Native American youth today, his innate wisdom, and his clear vision of the purpose of the collection raised this book to new levels.

Dr. Hap Gilliland, president of the Council for Indian Education, put us in touch with outstanding teacher Mick Fedullo. His students from Lodge Grass High School and Middle School in Montana submitted numerous wonderful pieces for consideration. Marjane Ambers, editor of *Tribal College, Journal of American Indian Higher Education,* disseminated information about the project all over the United States. At the Institute of American Indian Arts in New Mexico, Robin Jones spent countless hours working with and encouraging her students to take this opportunity to be published. James Graham, coordinator for the American Indian Education Program in Marysville, California, sent individual project announcements to all his young writers throughout the state. Peter Markus, a teacher in the InsideOut Writing program in Detroit, worked with his students to prepare their submissions. Ande Diaz and Alfred Bush from Princeton University went out of their way to find writers and put us in touch with valuable contacts. Chief Gregory E. Pyle helped tremendously to disseminate information throughout the Choctaw Nation. With the tireless help of Rebecca Dallinger of *New Voices* at The Circle in Minnesota, many midwestern writers were given the chance to submit. Poet and editor of *Feeding the Ancient Fires, A Collection of Writings by North Carolina*

American Indians, MariJo Moore, generously put us in touch with her talented writers in North Carolina. In Rita Sparling's classroom in Nevada and Rachel Stuy's classroom in Nunavut, Canada, Suzanne Williams conducted workshops and encouraged young writers to submit to the collection. Tim McLaughlin and Father Peter J. Klink, S.J., gathered submissions from Red Cloud School in South Dakota. In the early stages of the project, Wayne Grigsby of Friendship House in San Francisco lent his wholehearted support, as did Jean Frankenfeld in South Dakota. Thank you to Allison Hedge Coke, who encouraged her diverse group of students to submit their work, and to Julie Ross from the Montana Unified School District (Title IX), who helped gather submissions. Jodi Burshia of *Red Ink* at the University of Arizona worked with us closely to get the word about our project out to her writers, as did the people at Artsreach in Arizona — Kit McIlroy, Barbara Teso, and Joanna Hearne. Jaqueline Keeler suggested numerous contacts across the country. Throughout the project, Lee Francis, national director of Wordcraft Circle, lent his support.

Thank you to Jim Fisher at Fort Berthold Community College, Trish Reeves at Haskell Indian Nations University, Michael Spurgeon at DQ University, Charles Woodard at South Dakota State, Norma Wilson at the University of South Dakota, Janet Fyne Cochran at Guilford College, Barry Landeros-Thomas at Ohio State University, and Marcus Bakurza at Arizona State University. Denni Woodward and Margaret Azevedo at Stanford University and Laurie Alviso Alvord, Steven Abbott, and Michael Hanitchak at Dartmouth College all lent their support, as did Laura Wyth at Harvard University. Thank you to Marc Chavez at UC San Diego, to Luana Ross from the University of Washington, to Alexandria LaFaye at CSU San Bernadino and her student honorees, and to Bill Cumming, who put us in contact with Maureen Smith at the University of Maine. David Treuer at the University of Minnesota, Robert Reising at the University of North Carolina at Pembroke, and Jeff Hamley, Arthur Sze, and Jaime Smith at the Institute of American Indian Arts supported our work as well.

In the East, Dora Conte of Chimney Corners offered her assistance with submissions. Earl H. Mills, Sr., chief of the Mashpee Wampanoag Nation, and Terrie Drew at the North American Indian Center helped us gather submissions in Massachusetts. The Office of Indian Education (Title IX) in Washington, D.C., also put the word out on the East Coast.

In the Minnesota area, Josie Rawson gave us many valuable contacts. Joseph Bruchac, Maurice Kenny, Juanita Espinosa of the Native Arts Circle, Christi Atkinson of the Walker Art Center teen programs, Ann Brummel at the Circle of Life School, Jerod Santek of The Loft Literary Center, Al White at the Heart of the Earth School, David Williams, Loree Meltich, Diane Wilson of the *Minnesota Literature Newsletter,* Heid Erlich of Birch Bark Books, Mary Helen Pelton, and Vicky Overstar all helped with the project. In Ohio, Mitzie Verne and Esther Bockhoff spread the word. In Detroit, Terry Blackhawk of the InsideOut Literary Arts Project was very helpful in the early stages. Erik Torkelson from Lac du Flambeau School in Wisconsin also sent us submissions from his students.

Thank you to Linda Poolaw, who helped us in Oklahoma. We also appreciated support from Connie Krueger, Kathy Huse-Wika, Wendy Mendoza, and Beth Witt in South Dakota. Simone Ingram and Evelyn Acton had contacts in this area as well.

John Fox, author of *Poetic Medicine: The Healing Art of Poem-Making,* put us in touch with Lupita McClanahan in the Southwest. We were also able to locate young Southwestern writers thanks to author Daniel Powers, Uma Krishnaswami, Jim Mesher, Barbara Robidoux, Mr. Reardon, Leslie Ellen Dickens, Naomi Mudge, and Mary Bowannie.

In California, we would like to thank Jennifer Varencheck of the "Clubhouse," affiliated with United American Indian Involvement in southern California, Cowy Kim of *YO!* in San Francisco, Vignetta Charles of the American Indian Child Resource Center in Oakland, Peggy Lemke, Sherry Goky, L. R., Tina Ichord Johansson, Kathy Martinez, Gloria Evangelista, Colleen Larimore,

Tekla White, Sherry Smith, James Kass from Youth Speaks in San Francisco, Thomas Schellenberg, JoAnne Wetzel, Susan Elya, Karen Dean, Danielle Wohl, Ann Muench, Kris Aro McLeod, and the California Poets in the Schools organization.

Our Southern contacts included Derek Lowry and Yvonne Dial. In the Northwest, John Hagman spread the word about our project through his I'wa'sil program. We would also like to express our appreciation to the Federation of Saskatchewan Indian Nations.

Thank you to Maya Ochoa for reading the selections and giving her thoughtful feedback as an American Indian teenager, and to Marjorie Franco for her editing assistance. From the beginning to the end, Lorraine Bates Noyes, a writer, offered invaluable advice that was key to the success of the project and recommended young authors and contacts throughout the country. Maria Damon, a writer and professor at the University of Minnesota, provided constant support, and linked us with contacts throughout Minnesota and Massachusetts, which led us to a number of strong authors.

We are grateful to *Indian Country* for including our project description in their newspaper and to Classroom Connect for advertising for us online.

Thank you also to our editor, Mary Lee Donovan, and to Candlewick Press for their dedication to this book and for their support of another community-based book, which will include all the other authors who submitted, enabling everyone to be heard.

Thank you to everyone who encouraged us and helped us throughout the United States and Canada. You have a share in giving American Indian teenagers and young adults a chance to speak out on a national level.

Annette Piña Ochoa has been working with the Indian Education Program for the last ten years. She graduated from the University of California, Davis, with a degree in Native American Studies. Annette Ochoa was born in St. Helena, California, and her Yaqui ancestry is of the Piña family from Old Guadalupe in Arizona. Her desire is to see American Indian children discover their stories and realize their goals in life. She lives in California.

Betsy Franco writes picture books, children's poetry collections, and innovative educational books. Her more than fifty books include two anthologies written by teenagers: *You Hear Me? Poems and Writing by Teenage Boys* and *Things I Have to Tell You: Poems and Writing by Teenage Girls,* both named Best Books for Young Adults by the American Library Association. Betsy Franco finds that helping young writers get published complements her own writing. She lives in California.

Traci L. Gourdine is a published poet and short-story writer whose works have appeared in several national literary magazines. She is Professor of English at American River College, and Chair of Creative Writing for the California State Summer School for the Arts. Through the Arts in Corrections Program, she has facilitated creative writing workshops for men, women, and children incarcerated in California state prisons.

Simon J. Ortiz, Acoma Pueblo, has been writing for more than thirty years and has close to twenty books to his credit. In 1969, he received the Discovery Award from the National Endowment for the Arts. He has taught at numerous universities and institutions, and was a Fellow in the International Writing Program at the University of Iowa. In 1993, Mr. Ortiz received a Lifetime Achievement Award from the Native Writer's Circle of the Americas. "Most of my work," he says, "focuses on issues, concerns and responsibilities we, as Native Americans, must have for our land, culture and community." Simon J. Ortiz lives in New Mexico.

Sam English was born in 1942, the son of Sam English, a member of the Redlake Band of Chippewa Indians, Redlake, Minnesota, and Blanche Delorme English, a member of the Turtle Mountain Band of Chippewa Indians, Belcourt, North Dakota. Neo-Native Expressionism is a term used by some collectors to describe the work of Sam English. He believes his role is to paint the contemporary Native American in a spiritual sense. Mr. English has been honored with numerous awards from Native American art shows around the country, and has received approximately fifty commisions from various tribal, governmental, and nonprofit organizations. In 1997, he was commissioned by the Presidential Inaugural Committee to create a mural for the 1997 inauguration. Sam English is also a social activist on reservations and in urban Indian communities.

A note about the jacket image from Sam English

The spiritual man at the center of the image is passing the eagle upward, meaning our stories, poems, and ceremonies are being sent to the creator, to the spirit world for recognition. We are, of course, star people. Without the spiritual elders and the lore they pass on to us, we have no future. They provide the young with a foundation of American Indian integrity.

The four basic elements — air, mother earth, water, and sky — are represented in the painting because they must be respected, taken care of, and preserved if we are to have a future.